INVEST
LIKE A
SHARK

FT Press
FINANCIAL TIMES

In an increasingly competitive world, it is quality
of thinking that gives an edge—an idea that opens new
doors, a technique that solves a problem, or an insight
that simply helps make sense of it all.

We work with leading authors in the various arenas
of business and finance to bring cutting-edge thinking
and best-learning practices to a global market.

It is our goal to create world-class print publications
and electronic products that give readers
knowledge and understanding that can then be
applied, whether studying or at work.

To find out more about our business
products, you can visit us at www.ftpress.com.

INVEST

LIKE A

SHARK

**How a Deaf Guy with No Job and Limited Capital
Made a Fortune Investing in the Stock Market**

JAMES "REVSHARK" DEPORRE

Vice President, Publisher: Tim Moore
Associate Publisher and Director of Marketing: Amy Neidlinger
Executive Editor: Jim Boyd
Editorial Assistant: Pamela Boland
Development Editor: Russ Hall
Digital Marketing Manager: Julie Phifer
Publicist: Amy Fandrei
Marketing Coordinator: Megan Colvin
Cover Designer: Ingredient
Managing Editor: Gina Kanouse
Project Editor: Betsy Harris
Copy Editor: Gayle Johnson
Proofreader: Kathy Bidwell
Indexer: Erika Millen
Compositor: codeMantra
Manufacturing Buyer: Dan Uhrig

© 2008 by James DePorre
Published by Pearson Education, Inc.
Publishing as FT Press
Upper Saddle River, New Jersey 07458

Charts courtesy of TeleChart® which is a registered trademark of Worden Brothers, Inc., Five Oaks Office Park, 4905 Pine Cone Drive, Durham, NC 27707. Ph. (800) 776-4940 or (919) 408-0542. http://www.worden.com.

This book is sold with the understanding that neither the author nor the publisher is engaged in rendering legal, accounting or other professional services or advice by publishing this book. Each individual situation is unique. Thus, if legal or financial advice or other expert assistance is required in a specific situation, the services of a competent professional should be sought to ensure that the situation has been evaluated carefully and appropriately. The author and the publisher disclaim any liability, loss or risk resulting, directly or indirectly, from the use or application of any of the contents of this book.

FT Press offers excellent discounts on this book when ordered in quantity for bulk purchases or special sales. For more information, please contact U.S. Corporate and Government Sales, 1-800-382-3419, corpsales@pearsontechgroup.com. For sales outside the U.S., please contact International Sales at international@pearsoned.com.

Company and product names mentioned herein are the trademarks or registered trademarks of their respective owners.

Printed in the United States of America

Second Printing December 2007

ISBN-10: 0-13-221308-7
ISBN-13: 978-0-13-221308-0

Pearson Education Ltd.
Pearson Education Australia PTY, Limited.
Pearson Education Singapore, Pte. Ltd.
Pearson Education North Asia, Ltd.
Pearson Education Canada, Ltd.
Pearson Educación de Mexico, S.A. de C.V.
Pearson Education—Japan
Pearson Education Malaysia, Pte. Ltd.

Library of Congress Cataloging-in-Publication Data

DePorre, James.
    Invest like a shark : how a deaf guy with no job and limited capital made a fortune investing in the stock market / James "RevShark" DePorre.

    p. cm.

Includes index.
    ISBN 0-13-221308-7 (hardback : alk. paper)   1. Stocks.   2. Portfolio management.
3. Investment analysis.   4. Investments.   5. Stocks—United States.   I. Title.

HG4661.D47 2008
332.63'22—dc22

                                                                                2007021594

To my wife, Gail, and our children, Anneliese, James III, and our forthcoming new addition, Samuel. Everything I do is for you.

And in memory of my father, James Louis DePorre, Sr., whose love and support will never be forgotten.

Contents

Acknowledgments

This book is largely a product of my interaction with readers and members of SharkInvesting.com and RealMoney.com. I thank them for the honor of reading my many columns over the years and for taking the time to ask questions and discuss topics. Like all teachers, I've learned far more from you than you have from me.

There is none better than the SharkInvesting.com team of Brenda Bryant, Jim Koford, Samit Gala, Brian Dubil, Jay Brenchick, and JP Winkler. Thanks for your exceptional loyalty and daily support.

Special thanks go to the members of the Shark Tank Chat Room who have joined me in the market battle day after day for over seven years. The Shark Tank is my investing home, and I look forward to many more years together.

Thanks to Scott "Lizard King" Slutsky who has traded with me from the beginning. He has not only been a source of support and ideas but also has been a good friend.

Thanks to the folks at theStreet.com and RealMoney.com, in particular Dave Morrow, Tim Johnson, Bill Hennelly, Jim Duffy, and Jim Cramer, who work hard every day to produce, promote, and make sense of my columns.

Thanks to my agent Dan Mandel for his help and guidance.

Thanks to the team at Pearson. Jim Boyd, who approached me with the idea for a book and believed in it from the start, did an excellent job of pushing and prodding me when I needed it most. Thanks to Amy Neidlinger, Julie Phifer, Gayle Johnson, Betsy Harris, and the many others who did exceptional work making sure everything came together as it should.

It is the love and support of my wife, Gail; my children, Anneliese, James, and Samuel; my mother, Muzzy; my siblings, Jan, Barry, Martine, Susie, Christine, Yvette, and Leon; my in-laws, Jimmy and Norma; and my entire family that makes it all worthwhile.

About the Author

James L. "RevShark" DePorre is widely viewed as one of the nation's top stock market investment advisors and commentators. He is CEO of Shark Asset Management, Inc. and Shark Investing, Inc. He operates www.SharkInvesting.com, whose mission is to educate and empower individual investors. DePorre has been a featured writer for Jim Cramer's RealMoney.com since 2001. A pioneer in educating investors online, DePorre joined Herb Greenberg in 1995 to found AOL's The Shark Attack trading site, which quickly became a premier destination for serious traders. In 1999, he founded the first Shark Investing website, Supertraders. Since then, www.SharkInvesting.com has evolved from its chat room roots into a full-service financial content website.

Foreword

James "RevShark" DePorre is a rarity. He is one of the very few individual investors with no institutional experience who has made a mark in the investing world by sharing his unique insights into how small investors can make money in the stock market.

Over the last six years, Jim and I have been featured side by side on RealMoney.com. Over that time, we have had some prodigious—how shall I say—*discussions* on some finer points, but besides sharing a first name, we have something far more fundamental and important in common. We both want to teach you how you can beat the market and make lots and lots of money.

The book you are holding is, hands-down, one of the most original and insightful books I have ever read when it comes to teaching you, the individual investor, not only why you have the ability to beat the Whales of Wall Street, but also *how* you can do it. Jim came into this game at a time when all the rules were changing and was one of the first people to realize that the Internet had revolutionized the way in which anyone who wanted to could take control of their investing fate.

More importantly, however, was that he knew that, to generate real returns, investors would have to manage their money in a way that was completely different from the kind of approach they had taken as gospel. He instinctively understood that the pundits who held onto the notion that the only way to be successful in the market was to buy good stocks and hold onto them forever were doing their audience a great disservice.

Several years ago, I hung up my hat after a long run as a very successful hedge fund manager. I helped make a lot of very rich people even richer, but I was anxious to use my years of experience as an industry insider for a better purpose. I wanted to convey my knowledge of how Wall Street really works to millions of individual investors. When I managed other people's money, I *was* one of the Wall Street Whales that Jim talks about.

Jim DePorre has always approached the investing game as an outsider. He was a David in a sea of Goliaths, and was able to find their weaknesses and exploit them to his advantage. Jim has taken years of conventional wisdom, turned it on its ear, and imparts his lessons to you in this book.

I told you already that Jim and I have worked side by side for six years, but in fact, until the summer of 2007, we had never met face to face. You already know that I'm not a shy person or that I will never miss an opportunity to play my role as a shameless self-promoter (and if a few chairs get banged up in the process, then so be it). The thing you have to know, however, is that I am not so set in my ways that I can't understand that there's more than one way to make money in the stock market.

So, when we finally did have the chance to meet in person and work on a few things together, Jim was even able to convince me that a few concepts that I have held for years could use some, um, tweaking. You see, I made my fortune by making moves ahead of major shifts in the market, and I am pretty darn good at it. Jim, however, knows that you can greatly reduce your risk of losing money by reacting to what the big boys on Wall Street are doing. They leave their tracks all over the place, and if you know where to look and how to use that information, then you can profit very nicely without having to stick your neck out for a market thesis that may or may not come true.

This book is based on a goal that I strive to achieve every day on television, which is to help you make a lot of money. If you are a seasoned investor or if you have just come to the realization that many of the so-called professionals out there may not exactly have your best interests in mind when they give you their advice, then I suggest that you take some time out of your busy schedule and read this book.

Even if you have no interest in the stock market and are only reading this foreword because you have seen some of my antics on YouTube, this book is a great read. I'll let Jim give you the details himself, but let me just say that every Thanksgiving, I look forward to reading about how a guy who lost his hearing, his livelihood, and even his marriage was able to take the hand that Fate had dealt to him and, using nothing but the tools he had available to him as a small, individual investor, make a fortune.

Jim DePorre is engaging, he's personable, and he's a master at taking concepts that often seem like only people with very expensive calculators can understand them and communicating them to his readers in a way that is not only understandable, but also actionable. The thing that strikes me most about Jim is that, despite his success in the stock market and the fact that he now manages money for others, he has never taken his focus off of speaking directly to individual investors. He has taken years of experience and wisdom and has put them into one cohesive resource so you can use his methods yourself.

I am willing to bet that, deep down, all of you know that you can make money in the stock market, and that you should be able to do it without having to pay outrageous fees to a broker who just wants your business and doesn't care if you beat the market. What you have here is a handbook on using RevShark's own unique style of investing. Sure, he's learned from the successes and mistakes of others (and yes, we've all had our own share of those), but his method is unlike anything else you will find on the shelves stuffed with books dispensing the same old investment advice you might be standing in front of right now.

Even though our methods may differ, if you want to be a better investor and learn how to capitalize on your strengths, then you should read this book. Not only does Jim show you how to become a better stock picker, he also shows you why it is important to aggressively protect your capital. If you've ever watched my television show or read any of my books, you know that I will tell you that bulls make money, bears make money, but pigs get slaughtered. Trust me, you need to take the time to see what Jim has to say about not being a pig.

The bottom line is that Jim gives you an approach that allows you to use your own unique advantages as an individual investor, a way of understanding what is really moving the market on a day-to-day basis, and a system of managing your money that will keep you in the game and make you a much better investor. Without giving too much away, Jim is a master at understanding the emotions of market players and teaches you how to game the gamers.

Now let me climb out of the water and back onto the beach, dry myself off, and ask...are you ready to swim with the Shark?

James J. Cramer
August, 2007
New York, New York

Preface

Becoming totally deaf and losing my career and almost everything I owned is the best thing that ever happened to me. If these things hadn't occurred, I would never have discovered the amazing financial opportunities that the stock market holds for small, individual investors who approach investing in the right way.

What felt like a huge personal disaster from which I would never recover ultimately led me to develop an approach to the stock market that I call Shark Investing. Shark Investing seeks to protect capital while aggressively pursuing profits. It takes advantage of the quickness and great flexibility that small investors possess. Shark Investing helped me turn a small sum into many millions, and I'm confident that you can do the same.

This book tells you why Shark Investing is a superior approach to the market and sets forth the steps you can take to seize control of your investing fate. After you read this book, you will never look at the stock market in the same way again.

Part I

Turning the Tables
on Wall Street

1

Shark Investing: Empowering the Individual Investor

Most investors confront the stock market like minnows confront the ocean. If they are lucky, they swim around and enjoy a few snacks before they end up as a tasty meal for someone else. Individual investors have a tendency to relinquish control of their financial fate. They invest their money in what they think are good stocks or mutual funds and then do nothing other than hope and pray that the investment seas will treat them kindly. When they do act, they do so out of emotion and without any sort of plan or strategy.

Typically investors have little appreciation of the substantial risks they take with their hard-earned capital by being passive. They buy stocks that are considered "safe" or "blue chip" and then abandon control over the situation and wonder why they earn mediocre returns. They rely on hope and luck rather than skill or strategy and are gamblers rather than risk-averse speculators.

My personal experience in the stock market has proven that it is possible for investors not only to protect their capital and control their destinies but to flourish much like a shark in the ocean. The essence of my Shark Investing approach is to embrace the benefits of being a smaller investor by being more active and aggressive. The logic of moving quickly to protect your capital in a volatile situation is obvious. However, the vast majority of investors not only choose to remain passive and inactive in this always risky and uncontrollable market environment, but also have been brainwashed into thinking this is the best approach.

This naive thinking about the market is primarily a function of misleading traditional beliefs that most of us never question. In addition, the powerful forces that dominate Wall Street tend to have interests that are counter to our own. Wall Street professionals and the financial media have convinced investors that there is no way to successfully invest other than to follow the traditional methods. Not so coincidentally, these methods are very lucrative for big institutions and those dispensing the advice. (See Chapter 5, "Why Conventional Investment Advice Ensures Mediocre Results.")

Investors have had it pounded into them by Wall Street professionals that it is best to be inactive and forgiving when it comes to investments because, in the long run, things will likely turn out okay. Unfortunately, this conventional investment wisdom not only results in mediocre returns, but also carries an above-average risk of loss. Holding on to good stocks for the long term sounds great in theory. But when an investor holds on to the wrong stocks for the long term, the damage to his or her financial well-being compounds quickly. Compounding is a powerful financial tool that is the road to real wealth, but it cuts both ways and must be harnessed and controlled.

In most cases the traditional methods of Wall Street never even put investors into the best stocks to begin with. After the fact, we hear how profitable we would have been had we bought Microsoft, Intel, or whatever the big winner of the past might have been. Racking up big gains is always easy in retrospect, but financial advisors fail to tell us how difficult it is to pick a stock right now that has substantial potential and is worthy of being held for the long term. We earn lackluster returns while we seek out the big winners that we can hold for the long run. We also take the chance that our savings will erode if we pick the wrong stock and sit with it for years while we wait for it to produce.

Investors are lulled into passivity by pithy Wall Street sayings such as "Buy low, sell high," "Find good stocks and hold them for the long run," and "Don't try to time the market, or you will surely miss the big move." (See Chapter 6, "The Myths of Wall Street.") Brokers and financial advisors constantly reassure troubled investors that, if they remain patient and passive, the highly researched stocks, selected by their expert analysts, are sure to bounce back and go ever higher.

Investors are told not to worry when their portfolio is bleeding red ink. They are actively encouraged to just hold on because the market is sure to turn and it would be a big mistake to sell and lock in a loss. The message from financial advisors is that "real" investors rely on the courage of their convictions and stick with certain "quality" stocks through thick and thin. Wall Street makes individual investors feel that changing their minds and acting aggressively to limit losses will damn them to financial hell.

In the world of traditional Wall Street, lower prices are never a cause for concern. Investors never lose money. They only experience endless "buying opportunities." This is an excellent approach to the market as long as you have a never-ending stream of cash and an infinite time frame in which to wait for the payoff. But for those who live in the real world and who must deal with a steady diet of financial demands, the frustration of passively holding stocks that aren't doing well is tremendous.

Those catchy little investment aphorisms that are so blithely tossed around by financial professionals and the media do contain some elements of truth. It really is common sense to "hold on to good stocks." So we happily incorporate these trite and convenient ideas into how we approach the stock market and then incorrectly believe that we are doing the best we possibly can.

What else is the average investor to do? How can the lone investor beat the big, powerful Whales of Wall Street, who have superior information, huge amounts of capital, and the ability to manipulate what happens in the markets? The answer is that he or she must learn to exploit the very qualities that make the Whales so dominant. Individual investors must use the Whales' strengths and inherent characteristics against them and create their own advantage.

A small, savvy group of investors has learned how to do just that. They understand how and why Wall Street operates the way it does and have found ways to use their small size and quickness to benefit from it. They are solitary hunters who move quickly and decisively when the time is right. These investors are the Sharks, and this book teaches you their secrets.

Technology Empowers the Little Guy

Shark Investors have been around as long as there has been a stock market, but for many years they were an exceedingly small group that had close ties to Wall Street. Generally they were wealthy, well-connected individuals and not just the average guy off the street.

That all changed as investing tools and methods became available through the Internet. Technology now makes it possible for anyone who is willing to put forth the effort to be a Shark Investor. In the past, the average investor had no choice but to rely on brokers, financial advisors, and the media for insight into and advice about the investing process. That is no longer the case.

Over the last decade the explosion of computers, satellite and cable TV, high-speed Internet, specialized financial media, and websites has greatly changed the tools that are available to the average investor. It is now possible to live virtually anywhere in the world and have the same investing tools that only professionals on Wall Street had in the past.

Even with all this new and fantastic technology and information, most people continue to invest their hard-earned money in much the same way they did decades ago. Investors now have accounts with online brokers, access to an overwhelming amount of investment advice on the Internet, and 24-hour financial television. But they are still advised that the best way to approach the market is the same way their grandfathers did.

Why don't investors better use the modern tools that are available to them to improve their investment results?

There are two key reasons. First, many investors simply don't know how to use investment tools and information effectively. Many software applications, websites, and information sources are designed to help with investing tasks, but they are so overwhelming, complex, and inconsistent that people often feel even more confused and uncertain about how to proceed. Buried in this flood of information are the tools that make it possible for anyone to be a Shark Investor.

A good example of an extremely valuable tool that many individual investors are unfamiliar with are stock charts (discussed in Chapter 9, "Charts: Navigating the Market Seas"). Stock charts are very helpful in implementing a winning investment strategy. They provide insight and structure, but there is a tendency to overcomplicate their use and to consider them useful for only hyperactive traders.

Many on Wall Street go so far as to actively discourage investors from using charts. They are often dismissed as nothing more than useless voodoo. This brings us to the second reason that technology tools are not adequately used to improve individual investing. Wall Street has convinced investors that it is downright dangerous to ignore traditional advice.

Wall Street wants investors to stick with conventional investing methods that produce commissions and fees. They want the individual investor to leave funds in their hands and be dependent on them for advice. The Whales of Wall Street don't want aggressive, self-sufficient Investing Sharks to make waves in the investment sea. They want passive minnows who are totally dependent on them for costly and questionable advice.

The Whales of Wall Street

Wall Street is dominated by Whales. These are the giant mutual funds, pension plans, hedge funds, institutions, and brokers that trade the vast majority of volume on Wall Street every day. These entities aren't just big; they are huge and powerful and have the capacity to move the market when they are so inclined. On any given day, at least 80% of the volume of stocks traded on Wall Street is produced by the Whales.

The mistake that the vast majority of individual investors make is that they believe that the best way to invest is the exact same way the Whales of Wall Street invest. They strive to be miniature versions of giant funds. They use the same strategies and approaches that billion-dollar mutual funds employ. What is really surprising is that most investors are so indoctrinated by Wall Street that they believe they can actually beat the Whales by playing the investing game the exact same way the Whales play it.

What do you think the chances are that an individual, sitting at home with limited information, can find better investments than a fund that spends millions of dollars on research, has easy access to company management, and employs teams of people to dig into every aspect of a business?

Unless you are extremely lucky, trying to compete against a mutual fund by mirroring its techniques is not a strategy that will produce superior results. It is like challenging a sumo wrestler to a wrestling match. There is no chance of beating him at the thing he does best. However, if you challenged him to a foot race, a game of basketball, or something where his size is a disadvantage, your chance of success would be very high.

Sharks don't try to play the investing game the way the Whales of Wall Street do. That is futile and unproductive. Sharks approach the market in a way that allows them to capitalize on their speed, cunning, and flexibility.

A New Approach: Shark Investing

Few creatures have survived as long or as well as the shark. The shark, unlike his dinosaur cousins, continues to flourish. The reason is simple. The shark possesses a number of unique physiological and behavioral characteristics that keep it from danger and make it a highly efficient eating machine.

Sharks are cunning and aggressive. They rush in and feast on a good meal whenever they come across an opportunity. When conditions are right, they don't hesitate to gorge themselves in a feeding frenzy. They don't ponder theoretical matters and the state of the world. If there is something good to eat, they go after it and eat it.

Despite their aggressiveness and ferocity, sharks quickly swim away when circumstances change. They don't dawdle once they have their fill. They move on and start the hunt for the next opportunity. They are in constant motion, hunting, eating, swimming away, and then hunting some more. They are one of the most efficient hunters and survivors that have ever existed, and they are the perfect model for the individual investor who seeks to conquer the investment seas.

Investors have been led to believe that the best way to approach the market is to become a part of the vast school of other investors who, like tunas in the ocean, seek safety in the midst of thousands of other like-minded tunas. They are passive and have no real control over what happens to them. Their primary goal is to survive by following the crowd. Their passivity may keep them safe if they are lucky, but they are rewarded with unspectacular results and often end up as someone else's meal.

Shark Investing is about taking control of your investments. It is about being active and not passive. Sharks stalk their prey, move aggressively, and stay flexible but run when danger lurks. Sharks have no qualms about moving on to the next opportunity at the first sign of danger. They know that even the best situations will eventually become dangerous if they stay in one place too long.

One of the key benefits of Shark Investing is that it not only helps improve returns, but it also decreases the risk of loss. You minimize risk by learning to sell quickly and decisively, which is the investment equivalent of swimming away. If you are sitting in an unproductive investment, you dump it and move on. Selling is one of the most underrated and unappreciated tactical tools on Wall Street. Traditional Wall Street doesn't want you to sell. It will constantly find ways to talk you out of running for the safety and security of cold, hard cash.

To earn your fins as an Investing Shark, you have to be ready to reconsider much of what you think and believe about investing. Shark Investing is about harnessing your power as a fast-moving individual. One of the first things you will learn is contrary to popular market wisdom and just about everything you've ever read on the subject. Active investing, in which you stay in motion, is a far safer approach to the stock market than the long-term "buy-and-hold" approach that Wall Street promotes. (See Chapter 4, "Why Long-Term Buy-and-Hold Investing Is Far Riskier Than Shark Investing.")

Becoming an Investing Shark

The first step in becoming an Investing Shark is to understand the dynamics that are at work in the stock market. One of the primary reasons many investors struggle is that they have common misconceptions about the stock market and how it functions.

Investors don't really understand why stocks and markets move the way they do. They have incorporated the conventional thinking of the Wall Street Whales into how they think about the market. They fail to embrace the advantages that they possess over big funds and institutions. The first part of this book explores how Wall Street really operates and the thinking and theories that impact the market. A clear understanding of market dynamics will help you establish the thinking and theory behind Shark Investing. It also provides the foundation for developing an investing approach tailored to your unique circumstances.

Once you have mastered these concepts and have clarified how you think about the market, you can begin developing a Shark Investing strategy that is suitable for you. First we will discuss some basic Shark Investing concepts such as the use of charts (in Chapter 9) and a money management system (see Chapter 10, "Portfolio Management: The Key to Success").

The best Shark Investing style depends on your particular abilities, desires, and circumstances. After you master the thinking and foundational concepts of Shark Investing, you can adapt them in a way that works best for you. We will explore different stylistic choices in Chapter 12, "Developing Your Inner Shark."

As you commence your study of Shark Investing, keep one basic idea in mind: It is all about seizing control of your financial fate. Shark Investing requires that you spend some time and effort to understand it and apply it, but the rewards you gain for efforts can be life changing.

2

The Making of an Investing Shark

One hot summer day in Ann Arbor, Michigan, I was on the telephone with an IRS special agent, negotiating a settlement of a complex tax shelter scheme for a client. It was a messy situation, and after months of discussion, it looked like I was finally close to a favorable resolution. I was feeling pretty good about my work but was suddenly confronted with a major stumbling block that drove me close to outright panic.

The problem was that I couldn't understand anything the IRS agent was saying. The phone connection was fine, and the agent was speaking clear and proper English, but I couldn't understand her no matter how hard I tried. After years of trying to avoid the problem, I was now being forced to admit that I was deaf and could no longer do my job as an attorney.

I had struggled with minor hearing loss for most of my life. My mother and grandfather had similar problems, and I had apparently inherited the same faulty gene that was causing the hair cells in my cochlea, which enables hearing, to malfunction. My hearing loss had become gradually worse as I grew older, but it had never been bad enough to keep me from leading a normal life. I had obtained law and business degrees from the University of Michigan, had become a Certified Public Accountant, and had established a career as a tax and corporate attorney despite the problem. I frequently had to make minor accommodations for my hearing problem, such as sitting near the front of my classes and avoiding noisy places or rooms with poor acoustics, but it was seldom a major problem. Usually, my hearing problem was more often a source of embarrassment when I misheard something, rather than a major hindrance to my work and life.

That began to change dramatically on that summer day in the early 1990s. My hearing was now rapidly declining and becoming a major problem in all aspects of my life. I tried hearing aids, took lip-reading courses, and tried a variety of other ways to deal with it, but nothing much helped, and things steadily got worse. Eventually my hearing declined to the point where I was stone deaf. I could feel the vibrations from very loud sounds but heard nothing. I was incapable of carrying on a normal face-to-face conversation. Because I didn't know sign language or other deaf individuals, the only way I could communicate was via written notes.

Lawyers, even those who are also CPAs, who are unable to talk with their clients are not in demand. I was forced to close my law practice and some other fledgling business enterprises. I lost almost all my assets; even my floundering marriage dissolved. I was lonely, depressed, and almost broke, and I had no idea what I would do to support myself financially. Luckily, I had a small disability insurance policy through the State Bar Association that covered my basic living expenses, but the future looked awfully darn bleak.

I had no idea what I would do with the remainder of my life. My disability insurance would sustain me for a while, but without the ability to hear, there was virtually no meaningful work that I could do. Even the most menial labor required some communication skills. The chances of finding challenging and fulfilling work seemed extremely remote.

The resulting isolation was excruciating and felt insurmountable. I soon came to understand the answer that Helen Keller, who was deaf and blind, gave when asked which was worse. She responded "To be deaf is a greater affliction than to be blind.... Hearing is the soul of knowledge and information of a high order. To be cut off from hearing is to be isolated indeed."[1] My deafness had cut me off from the world, and I was lost.

While I struggled to figure out what I would do with my life, the technological marvel known as the Internet, which had been around for a while, rapidly began to become available to the average guy. I borrowed a personal computer from my brother-in-law, Fred, and started exploring early Internet services, such as Prodigy and CompuServe. In the online world the fact that I couldn't hear didn't matter much at all. I now could communicate with people via the computer about a multitude of topics. I had always enjoyed reading and now could chat about books and writing with other like-minded individuals. I explored sports, health, politics, and all sorts of other things that interested me. In some small way I no longer felt quite as isolated, but the problem of what to do with my life remained a daunting one.

Eventually, my travels on the Internet brought me to discussion boards on the Prodigy services that were dedicated to investing in stocks. These often trite, simplistic, and emotional discussions about obscure stocks turned out to be a major turning point in my life.

Previously, I had dabbled a bit in the market in the standard way—by consulting with brokers—but this was different. These people were doing their own research, were making their own decisions, and were not highly dependent on brokers or financial professionals. I had always been interested in the stock market and was intrigued by the possibility that I might be able to find a way to make some money in this manner.

I knew nothing beyond the most basic things about the stock market. Even though I had attended one of the best business schools in the country at the University of Michigan, only a few classes had dealt with investing in the stock market. Those classes primarily discussed the theory and ideas behind institutional portfolio management. No classes offered practical investment advice for the average individual that explored the various approaches to the market. Investing was done in one basic way in the academic world, and it wasn't very relevant to an individual investor working with a very small stake.

It was clear that if I wanted to learn how to make some money in the market, I had no choice but to teach myself. I had nothing else to do, so I dedicated myself to that task. In the early days few books, newsletters, websites, or resources provided any real insight into how the market worked. The resources that were available were mainly just variations of the same basic ideas about portfolio management and long-term investing that most everyone was familiar with. Nonetheless, I read everything I could find, thought about its validity, and tried to come up with ways to use the ideas to gain a real advantage in the market. The one thing that sank in was that if I followed the standard advice, I would end up investing like everyone else and had little chance of generating exceptional returns. I needed to find an approach that gave me an edge.

Every day I would read hundreds of posts on stock market message boards and contemplate the thinking and emotions that were involved. It became quite clear that, despite the bravado and bombast exhibited by many posters, individuals really didn't know how to effectively invest and optimize their profits. They were driven mainly by their emotions and were relying primarily on hope rather than some clearly defined insight or advantage. They would have some good luck at times and enjoy some nice gains, but few were rigorous or systematic in their approach, and I suspect their results were mixed.

By liquidating a retirement fund, selling some assets, and living frugally, I eventually managed to scrape together a stake of about $30,000. That was everything I had, and I could not afford to lose it, but I decided to give the stock market a try and see if I could find a way to make some money. Like many beginning investors, I was initially interested in small, speculative, unknown "story" stocks that were constantly talked about online. They have a get-rich-quick appeal and are hard to resist when you are working with small amounts and are trying to rack up some big profits very quickly. The stories always sound compelling and the risks minimal, but the reality is usually quite different.

Like most people, I lost quite badly on a few of these stocks. Some were outright frauds, and others look just plain ridiculous in retrospect. I realized pretty quickly that picking stocks based on stories and fundamental information would not give me any real edge. The average guy like me would never really know the truth about a company's prospects. I was simply playing the stock market equivalent of a slot machine. Even though I might eventually hit the jackpot, the odds were that I would lose most or all of my capital before I ever found the big winner. This approach to the market gave me no control over the eventual outcome. I had to put my money on the line and hope I was right. I realized I couldn't risk being so cavalier with my precious capital.

I continued to explore the possibilities, became increasingly active on the Internet stock boards, and tried a number of other approaches. Because I couldn't hear on the phone and there were no online brokers yet, I would drive to a broker's office and communicate with him via written notes about the stocks that interested me. Most of the time he would try to talk me out of what I intended to do and push me to buy stocks that the analysts at his firm had recommended. I assumed that these folks had superior information and insight, but more often than not the stocks performed poorly. The broker's response to my frustration was to suggest that I buy more, stay patient, and continue to hold on and wait for the inevitable payoff. Unfortunately, I found more and more of my precious capital tied up in stocks that were not doing that well. I had some small successes, but for the most part I passively sat and hoped that the stock gods would eventually reward me. The process gave me even less control over my money and left me feeling helpless when it came to controlling my financial fate.

It would have been easy to become disillusioned at this point, because even the advice of sophisticated market professionals apparently was of little value. If they couldn't do better than average, how could I possibly hope to? Despite this seemingly compelling logic, I refused to give up. I was just too intrigued by the possibilities I saw every day when I looked at the stocks that were making big moves. I was convinced that there had to be a better approach to the market, and I continued to shift my focus to gain control of my investing fate. Finally, slowly but surely, things started to fall into place.

The key realization for me was that I needed to be much more concerned with how a stock moved rather than the stock itself. Picking great stocks that didn't do anything wouldn't make me any money. I needed to latch on to stocks that were already in an upward motion and then move quickly to lock in gains should they stall. Every day stocks were making big moves, so why wasn't I focusing on them rather than the ones I hoped might make a big move someday?

My mistake was thinking that a small individual investor like me, with no connections or special resources, could find fantastic stocks that multibillion-dollar funds with huge staffs of researchers would miss. That doesn't happen very often. More often than not, I simply was wrong in my analysis of the stock. Even if I did find an exceptional stock, it didn't do much good if the market didn't embrace it as well. I could sit on a great stock for years and not realize any gains if the market didn't eventually discover what I had discovered.

So rather than trying to compete against big funds and institutions in hunting for good stores, I needed to focus on the stocks they had already found and were buying aggressively. Every stock had something positive to offer, but that didn't mean it would go up in price. That meant I had to focus on price movement. If a stock was going up on high volume, this probably meant that someone big with good information was buying and wanted to join that party.

I needed a way to track price, and that meant using stock charts. Charts removed the hope aspect of investing. I was no longer thinking about the story and what might happen at some distant point. I was forced to focus on the reality of price movement. If a stock had a good story or numbers but it wasn't moving, I figured I probably didn't know the full story. It seemed logical that there would always be someone out there with a lot more money and information than I had. So why fight them? They were big and well-informed, and they would determine how a stock moved, and it didn't much matter what I thought. These were the giant Whales of Wall Street, and they couldn't move without making some waves. It became pretty clear to me that if you looked at the charts you could track what these giants were doing. This was ideal for me, because I was just a little guy with a small amount of capital, and I could react quickly when I saw signs that the Whales were at work.

Rather than hoping that the market would uncover the great stock I had found, I could jump in and profit from the great stock that the big boys had already found. I didn't have to try to anticipate what might happen. Suddenly I was in control, because I was reacting and moving fast as circumstances changed rather than sitting and hoping and praying that things might work to my advantage.

Given my desire to have greater control over my investing and how precious my capital was, a reactive approach empowered me. I had shifted from focusing on the stocks themselves and now was centered on the action and investors who moved the stocks.

Focusing primarily on a stock's price action rather than the story of the company behind the stock was the first step in finding an approach to the market that provided me with a real advantage. The next step was focusing on the psychology and emotions that moved stocks. Although big institutions may determine a stock's longer-term course, the movement caused by swings in greed and fear often provided the best opportunities. More often than not, stocks moved in an irrational manner due to the influence of emotions. If you recognized that fact, many opportunities became apparent.

Things began to come together for me. I started finding a steady stream of good investments, and soon my initial stake had doubled and then tripled. The more success I had, the harder I worked at it, and soon my life was consumed by the stock market. The first online brokers were now appearing on the Internet, and that simplified the investing process greatly. Even CNBC added closed captioning to its broadcasts, so I could now "hear" what they had to say. Much of the technology available to investors was quite rudimentary back then, with slow dialup modems, delayed quotes, and limited news and data but it was becoming more readily available, and the prices were falling to very reasonable levels. I pretty much had everything I needed on my home computer to aggressively pursue the investing strategy I was developing, and that is exactly what I did.

As I began to clarify my investing approach, I posted my thoughts and comments on stock boards. To my surprise, a number of people were interested in what I had to say. I posted some stocks I liked and gave my suggestions on how to play them, and they worked out well. It seemed that I was developing a knack for this stock-market business. My temperament and intellectual abilities seemed well suited to playing the game. Frankly, I was just happy that I could talk and interact with people on the computer and not worry about my inability to hear.

By 1995 I was experiencing steady success with my methods. I would identify stocks that were moving, jump in and ride them for a while, and then jump out as soon as they began to falter. Most of my big winners turned out to be rather obscure small stocks that were not widely known. It became clear to me that if I were to make big money by investing, it wouldn't happen by buying the big, well-known names. I needed to focus on smaller, faster-moving stocks that were under the radar. Although these stocks carried more risk, they also offered much greater rewards, and if I was always ready to sell them, I could control my risk to a great degree.

A good example of the type of stock that I was finding is Wireless Telecom. During 1994 and 1995 the stock split several times as it increased tenfold (see Figure 2.1). I knew very little about the stock other than the fact that it was going up at a furious pace, but that was all I needed. I jumped into the fray and rode it but was always ready to hit the sell button should it begin to falter.

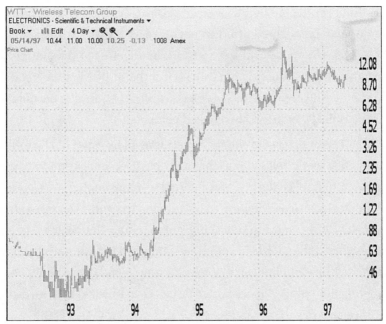

Chart courtesy of TeleChart® by Worden Brothers, Inc. www.worden.com

FIGURE 2.1   Wireless Telecom.

I continued to be quite active in discussing stocks like WTT on the Prodigy Service. One day two brothers named Tom and David Gardner, who eventually became known by the name the Motley Fool, popped up on Prodigy. They made quite a fuss as they tried to tell people how it wasn't possible to make money with active investing, and that buy and hold was the only way to go. I found their manner condescending and their theories questionable, but they provided an excellent outlet for debating the theories I was forming.

The Motley Fool's basic sermon was that investing was fairly simple. All you had to do was copy Warren Buffet by buying good stocks and holding them for the long run. Having tried this for many years, I questioned how simple this really was. The Fool relied heavily on sweeping generalizations and painted everyone who approached the market in an aggressive manner as blithering idiots who were wasting their time producing below-average returns. As the market climbed, the popular press also started to portray aggressive investors as wild risk takers who made and lost fortunes in a matter of days or weeks. Certainly there were individuals who did that, but what was ignored were methodical, risk-averse people like me who protected capital by moving quickly and steadily realized gains.

I had been slowly developing my skills as an investor. My brokerage statements were telling me that the passive, long-term investing approach that folks like the Motley Fool were promoting was a recipe for mediocre results. I felt it was my mission to spread the word about Shark Investing, and I adopted the screen name Rev Shark. My goal was to preach the merits of active investing and to save souls from the dangers of buy and hold. My point was simple and compelling. Shark Investing not only produces better results than buy and hold investing, but it can do so with much less risk.

America Online and the Motley Fool site eventually began to replace Prodigy as the central gathering point for online investors. To contain my constant debate and endless criticism of their passive approach, the Motley Fool eventually set up a board for "Active Investors" on which I could talk about the Shark Investing approach without the constant dogma of the buy-and-holders. This board became a haven for the steadily growing contingent of online traders. Even professional money managers like Jim Cramer were frequent readers, and many great ideas were shared.

In 1995 the Motley Fool began writing about a little stock called Iomega (IOM:Nasdaq). This stock gained wide attention and became one of the first great momentum stocks of the Internet era. I made huge amounts of money trading this stock as it was pushed higher and higher by frenzied emotions (see Figure 2.2). I posted many comments about the IOM chart and the power of momentum, and more and more people become intrigued by what I had to say.

IOM - Iomega Corp
COMPUTER HARDWARE - Data Storage Devices ▼
Book ▼   Edit   3 Day ▼
05/27/97 42.83 43.75 41.88 43.13 +0.30   5202 NYSE   Optionable +0.70%

88.42
56.73
36.39
23.35
14.98
9.61
6.17
3.96
2.54
1.63
1.04

JAS OND   94   AMJ JAS OND   95   AMJ JAS OND   96   AMJ JAS OND   97   AMJ T M L

Chart courtesy of TeleChart® by Worden Brothers, Inc. www.worden.com

FIGURE 2.2   Iomega.

A *San Francisco Chronicle* business journalist named Herb
Greenberg also operated a site on America Online. Herb was constantly bashing the fundamentals of IOM and talking about how it
was eventually doomed. I went after Herb mercilessly for his inability
to understand that this was a great investment for fast-moving Sharks
who understand the nature of momentum. There was big money in
chasing the stocks, and you could profit greatly by going along for the
ride. I tried to point out how the fundamentals were irrelevant when
emotions were swirling, but that approach was uncomfortable for
folks who focused on things like balance sheets and sales.

Herb, of course, was eventually proven correct about Iomega's ultimate fate. However, I and many other Shark Investors made a huge
amount of money trading the stock as it ran up and then collapsed.

Herb was different from most business journalists, and he appreciated my opposing point of view. He just didn't think my approach was suitable for most people. Despite my vitriol and differing viewpoint, Herb invited me to join his AOL site and enabled me to set up the Shark Attack short-term trading forum. This site became home to many very active market players during the late 1990s as the online trading world started to boom.

Needless to say, being an aggressive momentum trader in the halcyon days of 1997 through the top in March 2000 turned out to be very lucrative. My starting stake of about $30,000 had grown substantially, and I was producing investing profits approaching a million dollars a year. The bubble years were ideal for my methods, and profits continued to roll in. But what really made the biggest difference for me was that I had learned how extremely important it is to protect profits. When the bubble burst in the spring of 2000, I managed to hold on to most of my profits and then adapted as a much more difficult market environment emerged.

Everyone was a genius in the bull market of the late 1990s. All you had to do was buy and hold on as the market went straight up, but the ability to make a transition after the bubble burst was what determined ultimate success. After March 2000, you could no longer count on the bull market to bail you out of bad investing decisions. You could no longer throw money at high-flying technology stocks and simply wait for it to multiply.

When the market began to fall apart, the disciplined money management techniques I had developed helped protect me. I never allowed losses to run, I stayed diversified, and I refused to give back profits. I protected my capital before all else, and it paid off. I stuck with the simple chart-reading methods I had developed and continued to focus on smaller- and mid-cap stocks. Despite the downtrend in the indices, 2000 turned out to be my best trading year ever, and 2001 was not far behind.

Through the difficult years following the popping of the bubble in 2000, I continued to plod along, making steady progress and building my capital, with only minor setbacks along the way. I have continued to develop my investing strategy and philosophy and have sought to empower individual investors seeking greater control over their financial well-being.

In 2002 I began writing a column on RealMoney.com about investing that is geared primarily toward the individual investor. I also launched the SharkInvesting.com website, where I demonstrate my theories with a real money portfolio and provide a wide variety of educational material.

After many of years of managing just my own accounts, I relented in September 2005 and launched Shark Asset Management to manage funds for others. In January 2006 I launched a hedge fund and am gaining a whole new appreciation of the many advantages that the average individual investor enjoys.

My personal life took a turn for the better when I met a sweet, attractive woman who lived near my parents' vacation home in Florida. She was willing to learn some rudimentary sign language so that she could communicate with me. In 1995 we were married, and now we have a daughter, a son, and another child on the way.

To make things even brighter, a new development called a cochlear implant became available to me. About six years ago, I had the surgery, and it greatly restored my hearing. It isn't perfect, but I can carry on conversations and function normally in most situations.

I continually give thanks for how a personal tragedy turned out to be a blessing in disguise. If I had not lost my hearing, I probably would have never discovered the world of the stock market. Because I became deaf, I have made far more money than I ever imagined, greatly enjoy what I do, and have a wonderful family to share it with.

No matter how great your problems may be, or how bleak your life may feel, it is truly amazing how well things can eventually work out. I never thought it possible that I could be so successful, but it happened—and it can happen to you too, if you stay positive and don't give up.

Endnote

1. Jean Christie, "Keller, Helen" in the *Gallaudet Encyclopedia of Deaf People and Deafness* (New York: McGraw-Hill, 1987, vol. 2, p. 125).

3

What Is Shark Investing?

Shark Investing is an approach to the stock market designed to capitalize on the many unique attributes and advantages that the smaller investor possesses. Shark Investors use their small size, quickness, and aggressiveness to outmaneuver and outrun the Whales of Wall Street. Sharks seize control of their destiny. Not only are they quick to act when the time is right, but they are quick to retreat at the first sign of trouble.

Shark Investors employ a number of specific strategies, actions, and approaches, such as using charts and money management to time entries and exits (as discussed in detail later in this book). Above all else, Shark Investing is a mind-set. It is recognizing and understanding that as an individual investor you need to look at the market differently to gain an advantage. You must embrace the fact that there is no way you can consistently beat the Whales of Wall Street at the investing game by acting like a miniature Whale. Once you recognize that fact and start focusing on the advantages you have as a small individual investor, you will be on the road to investment success.

The first step in your journey to becoming an Investing Shark is to have the right attitude and mind-set. Shark Investors are empowered and gain confidence because they realize that they will no longer be pushed around by powerful forces that can't be controlled. Shark Investors think about investing very differently than big institutions,

mutual funds, and traditional brokers. If you make the Shark way of
thinking your own, the Shark Investing strategies and the reasons for
them will become second nature, and you will be able to act with confidence and certainty in the market.

The nine key characteristics of the Shark Investors have a number
of overlaps, but together they form a coherent theme that helps make
clear the proper course of action:

- Sharks are aggressive.
- Sharks are opportunistic and reactive.
- Sharks stay in motion.
- Sharks plan their attacks.
- Sharks are patient while they stalk their prey.
- Sharks take advantage of the emotions of the crowd as it
  becomes frenzied and emotional.
- Sharks don't have emotional or sentimental attachments to the
  stocks they profit from.
- Sharks are risk-averse and do not hesitate to swim away the
  moment they sense danger.
- Sharks have an attitude.

The following sections discuss each characteristic in detail.

Sharks Are Aggressive

Standard Wall Street investing methodology is to find an interesting
stock, do some careful fundamental research to be sure that it is a
good value, and then buy it and wait patiently for the big payoff a few
years down the road. That certainly sounds like a logical approach,
and it doesn't seem all that difficult. Although the theory sounds
good, you probably wouldn't have bought this book if you have been
wildly successful with such an approach.

The problem with that style of investing is that you relinquish control over the situation when you come to trust that your investment will work out over the long run. You might get lucky and pick the right stock, but there is a good chance that you won't. Your success is largely a function of luck rather than any action you might take.

Sharks don't count on luck. They seize control of their investments by being aggressive. When they see a good opportunity, they pounce and take advantage. When they have a good profit, or if things don't work out as they should, they dump the stock and move on.

The most successful Shark Investors understand that selling is one of their most powerful strategic tools, and they aren't afraid to use it. Many market players have elevated selling to such monumental status that they invoke it in only the most extreme circumstances. Shark Investors view selling in the opposite manner. It should be embraced and used frequently and often. The mantra of a typical Shark Investor is "When in doubt, get out."

The reason that aggressive selling is so important is that if you are willing to be aggressive when it comes to selling, it is much easier to be aggressive when it comes to buying. If you quickly cut your mistakes instead of holding on to them when they develop into major problems, you are likely to make more buys. The more buys you make, the better your chances of hooking on to some big winners.

In the stock market, it pays to constantly test the waters. If you take enough small probing bites, you will eventually find a tasty meal. If you are willing to sell quickly if things aren't right, there is little cost to doing so. Aggressive buying provides you with increased opportunities. Aggressive selling limits the cost of trying the opportunities.

Aggressiveness isn't limited to buying and selling. It also is important when it comes to finding good opportunities. The more good opportunities you have to aggressively buy and sell, the greater your chances of success. Too many investors keep going back to the same old stocks and miss out on major opportunities as shifts in the market occur.

Shark Investors constantly seek out new opportunities. They don't sit passively and hope a good idea will swim by. They develop strategies and methods that provide them with a steady diet of ideas that can be pursued aggressively.

Sharks are always ready to move aggressively. It is that willingness to act decisively and confidently that puts them in control of their investment returns.

Sharks Are Opportunistic and Reactive

Shark Investors focus on what is in front of them. If they see something they like, they go after it. If they see something that troubles them, they go in the other direction. They pounce on opportunities as they arise and react to danger as it occurs. They constantly look for investment opportunities and actively seek them out.

The Whales of Wall Street tend to be anticipatory. Because they are big and slow and unable to be aggressive, they tend to move into situations prematurely and then hope they will eventually play out in the desired manner. Shark Investors know that the best odds for profitable investments come not from anticipating market turns or changes in circumstances but from aggressively catching the meat of a trend after it starts.

Most traditional market players come to believe that success in the market comes from accurately predicting how the future will unfold. Although that can certainly make for some profitable investments when you are correct, there is no way to do it systematically and regularly.

Predicting the market's direction is an inexact science. No one, and I mean no one, has ever been able to do it consistently over the course of many years. A few market pundits have gained a measure of fame by predicting a crash, but none of them have ever done it more than once. In most cases, the great prognosticators of the past are considered jokes today. Lots of folks get lucky and occasionally make correct market calls, but no one can do this on a regular basis over the long term.

Individual investors shouldn't waste their time playing the prediction game. They are far better off moving quickly when something actually happens, rather than making bets on their ability to predict how the future might unfold. If even the most seasoned market professions are incapable of predicting the market's future twists and turns, how can lone individual investors possibly do it?

Shark Investors react to changes in the market. When a particular market opinion is actually reflected in the market action, that is the time to move. There is no logic in moving today when you anticipate that something might occur next week. If and when the event does occur, Shark Investors are small and fast enough to join in early enough to profit.

The one great absolute of the stock market is that it goes through alternating cycles of strength and weakness. A lot of folks make their living trying to predict when those shifts might occur. If you predict that the market will pull back, you will eventually get it right, but that isn't much of a prediction unless there is some precision to the timing. More money is probably lost waiting for predictions to be proven correct than is made when they do occur. Sharks don't play that game. They stick to what they see in front of them and react quickly as things change.

The Investing Shark knows that calling a market turn once in a while may make you a media hero, but reacting quickly to changing circumstances will make you rich.

Sharks Stay in Continuous Motion and Are Always Looking for Their Next Meal

Sharks never stop their quest to fill their bellies. They are always thinking about where they might find their next meal. They aren't content just because they had a good meal last night. They continue to hunt in the same methodical and aggressive manner.

Traditional investors have a tendency to limit their hunt for opportunities to the familiar. Dear old Dad owned IBM for many years, and you use Microsoft Windows at work, so you buy those stocks. That is easy and convenient and feels safe. It also frees you of the hard work of finding something better.

It isn't that investors are lazy about finding opportunities. Most simply don't know how to go about it. They might get an idea from television or a magazine, but they don't approach the hunt for stock market opportunities in a systematic way. If they occasionally stumble on to something, they are happy.

Investing Sharks look for new opportunities every day. When they find a good one, they do not hesitate to let go of old positions and grab on to the new. Market success is a function not only of making the right moves, but also of having the right stocks in order to make them. It doesn't do you much good to have an ideal investing approach if you don't have some good stocks to use that approach on.

The thrill of the hunt for the next big market winners is one of the most enjoyable aspects of the stock market. Investing Sharks spend time developing hunting methods and make this part of their routine. To a great extent the key to good investing is having a constant source of new ideas. Many investors fail to produce good results simply because they have a hard time dropping stocks that have rewarded them well in the past and embracing new and better ideas.

Investing Sharks are not only in constant motion looking for ideas. They are in continuous motion because you can't be successful in the market unless you are actually doing something. The ability to grab opportunities while others mull over the big picture and the meaning of various events is what separates the successful Investing Shark from the pack.

We need to study and understand the forces that move the market, but we can't allow analysis to keep us from action. It is only through action that we prosper. We never will eliminate all risks, no matter how hard we try, so sometimes we must simply act and risk the consequences. The easiest thing to do is nothing, so that is what people tend to do. They miss out on opportunities as a result.

Market success is a function of constant daily effort rather than doing nothing and then suddenly trying to hit a home run.

Sharks Plan Their Attacks

Successful Investing Sharks don't just buy and sell stocks randomly. They formulate specific strategies for each of their investments. They know when they want to buy, and they have a plan for when they will exit. They might not know exactly at what prices they will do such things, but they know the conditions that will trigger their moves.

The cruel nature of the stock market is that it seldom does exactly what we anticipate. Even when we prepare for multiple scenarios, the Stock Market Beast has a way of coming up with something new and creative that we hadn't contemplated. That doesn't mean we should forego strategic planning. The process of planning is extremely valuable even if you never use your plans. Imagining how events will play out and the market's reaction to them makes it much easier to react when events unfold. Developing a mind-set in which you understand the market's dynamic nature and are ready to amend your course of action as events unfold can pay off big.

One of the easiest traps for investors to fall into is to simply let their stocks languish because they don't really have any plan in mind. If a stock doesn't do what we want, rather than dump it quickly like we should, we just let it sit there. Sharks always have a plan and know what they are going to do, so that losses by inertia don't pile up.

Even if you never use your plans, the process of developing them ensures you don't let problems fester and grow. Having the mind-set to develop and implement strategic plans will make a huge difference in your investing results. You never know what will happen in the heat of battle, but if you are mentally prepared for anything, you have a big advantage.

Sharks Are Patient While They Wait for Opportunities

Aggressiveness and patience are not conflicting forms of behavior. It is possible to be both extremely patient and very aggressive—you just don't do both at the same time. The essence of patience is waiting until the time is right and not letting anxiety drive you to act prematurely. The essence of aggressiveness is bold and forceful action when the time is right. The combination of the two traits is extremely powerful.

Patience is important not only in waiting for the right opportunities to buy, but in waiting for the positions you have to eventually work. We can't expect the market to always be immediately cooperative. In fact, we should assume that it won't be and take that into consideration when planning our attacks.

We have to be prepared to sit and wait for long stretches and then act quickly and aggressively when the time is right. This can be a hard transition to make. Those who are adept at staying patient often have a hard time acting boldly, and vice versa. Many of us have a hard time resisting the itch for action. We anxiously anticipate what will happen in the future and find ourselves implementing our battle plans before the time is right. We use up our ammunition, and then, when Mr. Market is most vulnerable, we are incapable of taking advantage.

Even if you consider yourself a highly active investor, patience is a virtue you need to cultivate. That doesn't mean you do nothing; it means you make plans, plot strategy, stay vigilant, and prepare to attack when the time is right. You might test the waters now and then, but if you conserve your cash ammunition wisely, you will profit when the battle begins in earnest. Patient aggressiveness is one of the Investing Shark's greatest tools.

Sharks Feed Best in the Middle of a Frenzied Crowd: Trend Following

A hungry shark likes a crowded beach. Sharks don't sit in the middle of the ocean waiting for opportunities to come to them. They seek out action and are drawn to movement. Because Investing Sharks are small, aggressive, and fast-moving, they aren't afraid to jump into the middle of a frenzied crowd. They take advantage of the many great opportunities that pop up when the crowd is excited. They fill their bellies while they can and leave only after they have gorged themselves or when signs of danger begin to appear.

Sharks realize that the market waters vary tremendously. There are wide variations in the number of good opportunities that exist at particular times. Sharks take advantage of the good times and are content to do little when times are rough.

Shark Investors' approach to the market is basic. They want to be holding many investments when things are going up, and they want to be holding mostly cash when things are going down. They don't care if they are in the market at the exact moment when a move starts or ends; they just want to be there when a trend is in place. They want to catch the meat of a move and enjoy the good times while they can. They don't overanticipate the end, but they do appreciate the fact that the market cycle will turn and that they need an exit plan.

Probably the most disparaged entity on Wall Street is the "crowd." The great mass of ordinary investors is widely regarded by Wall Street professionals as being just downright dumb and inevitably wrong. Billions of dollars are traded by high-powered hedge funds on the belief that the crowd is always wrong.

The irony of this negative view of the crowd is that the crowd of investors is right most of the time. The market wouldn't go up if the great mass of investors weren't all thinking the same thing. Only when behavior becomes extreme does the wisdom of the crowd begin to break down.

Sharks want to run with the crowd because that is where the opportunities are. Because we move fast, we don't have to worry about the unsustainable extremes that inevitably occur. In fact, bubbles like the market experienced in the spring of 2000 can be hugely profitable for Shark Investors who go along for the ride and then swim away when early signs of problems pop up.

The crowd provides Shark Investors with many great opportunities. When the crowd is in control of the market, we go along for the ride, but when thing begin to turn, we don't hesitate to shift our direction and go against the tide to protect our gains and seek further profit.

Sharks Have Little Loyalty and Are Quick to Turn on Old Friends

Many investors have a tendency to become emotionally involved with their financial investment. They have not only money on the line but also feelings of competency and self-worth. For a very large group of investors, stocks aren't just vehicles by which they make or lose money. Stocks become friends and members of the family. Even when they act badly and disappoint us, we still love them and nurture them and hope things will eventually improve. They are viewed not only as a means to some financial end but as a referendum on us as individuals.

It isn't only individual investors who suffer from this sort of emotional attachment. Seasoned pros can be even more susceptible to it, because they often become so heavily invested in terms of both money and time that they couldn't extricate themselves even if they wanted to. Hence, they repeatedly find justifications to hold on to a stock.

Shark investors do not become emotionally attached to stocks. Just because a stock may have treated us well in the past doesn't mean it deserves loyalty. Loyalty to a stock is almost always misplaced and leads to making poor investing decisions. Once you begin thinking about a stock in terms of how well or badly it has treated you, there is great danger of ignoring what is actually happening.

If you had brief involvement with a good stock and enjoyed the experience, that doesn't mean you have to marry it. Perpetual dating might not be emotionally or psychologically fulfilling, but it can be the most lucrative approach in the market. Sharks know that the reason that big funds always warn us that "past results are not indicative of future performance" is because it is true. Just because a stock or market has done well in the past doesn't mean it will continue to do well.

Shark Investors have to constantly remind themselves to stay objective when evaluating the justifications for holding this stock. They want to make sure they are not letting emotional factors influence their thinking. If you didn't already own this stock, would you be inclined to be as heavily invested in it as you are now? You have to be tough on yourself when contemplating the real reasons you are holding on to a stock. After a while, inertia sets in, and you can end up holding, not because there is a good reason to, but because it is simply easier to maintain the status quo.

It is always interesting to look at the discussion about a stock of interest on the stock market discussion forums at locations such as Yahoo.com. You probably won't learn a whole lot, but you will be reassured that most investors are in no danger of becoming objective evaluators of stocks. Emotions dominate. That is a good thing for Investing Sharks, because those emotions help create opportunities.

What is most striking about the discussions on the Internet is the inflexibility of the views. Most of the postings are dominated by a core group of "true believers" who slice, dice, and dissect every trivial matter they stumble across. These folks are generally so heavily invested, both financially and emotionally, that even if they admit there is something negative about the stock, they still hold onto it. They are so intimately involved in it that they can't bring themselves to cut the ties that bind.

Every stock board also seems to have a bearish crank who delights in tormenting the true believers. The negativity that such cranks exhibit seems to have little to do with an objective analysis of the company itself, but is more of a psychodrama of some sort. Neither the true believers nor the cranks seem capable of effectively evaluating a stock's prospects. The true believers end up reassuring each other when things are breaking down, and the critics increase their taunting about how the good times end when the action is positive. Ultimately, these fanatics almost always push stocks to unrealistic levels, and that is good for the opportunistic Shark.

The moral of the story is that Investing Sharks don't become emotional about stocks or the market. They don't get attached negatively or positively, and they keep an open mind. They cultivate the attitude that the only good stock is one that makes them money and acts well. They don't waste time or effort looking for reasons to justify bad behavior. All stocks will eventually turn on you, and the moment they do, they no longer deserve your love, loyalty, or emotions.

Sharks are in the business of using stocks for one reason: to make money. If they aren't doing that, they should be bid adieu and tossed overboard without regret. If you want a friend, buy a dog. Save your emotional attachments for the people in your life that you care about.

Sharks Are Risk-Averse and Don't Hesitate to Swim Away When Danger Lurks

Successful Shark Investors must possess traits that seem quite contradictory. As discussed, Shark Investors must be decisive, aggressive, patient and confident when they see opportunity. However, they must also be able to change their minds quickly and run for safety if it looks like their initial decision was a bad one or if conditions change.

Unfortunately, human nature is such that it is difficult for most people to embody these seemingly conflicting attitudes. Those who are decisive often have a hard time admitting mistakes and then moving with confidence in a different direction. Those who can change their minds quickly often lack the sort of conviction that allows them to profit big when they are correct.

Some of the best investors may seem almost manic-depressive. One day they aggressively buy and act like the market will never go down again. A short time later they are negative and acting like the world is coming to an end.

Those quick swings from one firm opinion to a totally different one can be unsettling to the casual investor, but it is exactly this trait that many of the best investors possess. When they make a decision, they feel no uncertainty. They act aggressively and with great vigor. However, they have no qualms about quickly reversing themselves if they think they are wrong or if conditions change. The ability to make a clear decision, act on it boldly, and then change your mind seems almost schizophrenic at times, but it is a key element of how Sharks survive and proper.

When the market is at a point where it could easily roll over or produce another leg up, and there are good arguments to be made for either scenario, the easy thing is to sit back and do very little. The great investors, on the other hand, are inclined to make a decision and then are prepared to change their minds should things develop to show that they were wrong. When I believe the news flow is problematic and the technical picture is vulnerable, my inclination is to sell. I have no qualms about changing my mind and switching to a more positive posture should I see good reasons to do so. Learning how to be decisive and act aggressively while maintaining the ability to change your mind quickly is a difficult balancing act but one that is central to great success in the market.

Sharks Have an Attitude

Above all else, Shark Investing is primarily the cultivation of a certain attitude and mind-set. It is the realization and acknowledgment that if you want to succeed in the market, you have to seize control of your investing results and not let your destiny be determined by the vagaries of the market or the thinking of "professionals." You can't just sit back and hope that things will work out. You take control of your own well-being. It is possible that a passive approach to the market might work, but it is dangerous, extremely risky, and nothing more than gambling. Shark Investors don't hope; they act.

After you have fully integrated the Shark Investing mind-set, the market takes on a very different look. No longer is it an uncontrollable beast that pushes you around as it pleases. You suddenly have control. If you see opportunities, you waste no time on worthless evaluation. You jump on them and tear off a big tasty bite. If the market is uncooperative, you sell, swim away, and patiently wait for better opportunities to bubble up. Sharks know without a doubt that the market will offer a steady stream of investing meals. You simply stay patient and keep looking, and sooner or later you will profit again.

The most empowering thing about Shark Investing is realizing how wrong and misleading traditional investing advice is and always will be. The fact that so many people will never escape its clutches is a major positive for Shark Investors, who will benefit from the chum these people become.

Sharks are one of the oldest living complex organisms on Earth because they are masters at adapting to the world in which they live. They control what happens to them and do not leave their destiny and well-being in the hands of others.

Conclusion

The logic of Shark Investing is simple. It is to take control of your own well-being rather than letting market forces push you where they please. It is simply using the strengths and advantages you have as a flexible and fast-moving individual investor.

But theory is one thing. Putting these concepts into practice and using them and living them is the key. Knowing something and actually doing it are worlds apart. Now that you have embraced the theory and thinking of Shark Investing, we will study market dynamics and then delve into the nuts and bolts of making the approach work. As you do that, make sure you consider the traits we have discussed here and understand how they ensure your ultimate investing success.

Part II

Understanding the Way the Market Really Works

4

Why Long-Term Buy-and-Hold Investing Is Far Riskier Than Shark Investing

Suppose you were trying to figure out the best way to generate superior long-term returns in the stock market, and you listened to the popular investment media, big brokerage houses, and traditional wisdom. You would probably believe that the best approach is to emulate Warren Buffett. He is one of the richest people in the world and must be doing something right, so why not try to copy the way he invests?

The theory behind his success is to buy stock in very good companies at a very early stage and then hold on for the very long term while the investment multiplies many times. What Buffett actually did and how he became so wealthy is much more complex than this theory. In the early days, it involved using large amounts of leverage through the present-day equivalent of a hedge fund and things such as private placements that most of us can't readily duplicate. But the basic theory is a compelling one. Holding the stock of great companies for the very long term and watching your money compound is such a logical, simple, and easy approach to investing that any rational person would believe it is the only way to go.

The big problem with this approach becomes clear when you try to put the theory into practice. Most anyone can tell you what stocks have been the big winners in the past and impress you with how rich you would have become if you had bought them. For example, you could have bought a share of Microsoft for the equivalent of about 25 cents in 1987. The stock is now worth about $25, so your investment would have increased 100-fold. That means a $10,000 investment would now be worth a hefty $1,000,000. That sure sounds like a simple and easy way to get rich, doesn't it? Let's just buy 40,000 shares of the next Microsoft today when it is at 25 cents, hold on for the next 20 years while it goes up 10,000%, and then retire with a million dollars in profits.

Legions of investors try to do just that every day, and the vast majority fail. It isn't because they are poor investors, lacking in information, or approaching it in the wrong way. It is just a very hard thing to do. That is why we aren't overrun with thousands of Warren Buffetts who made their fortunes by holding on to a handful of stocks for decades. Mr. Buffett is a bright and glaring exception in the world of investing. To think that you can easily copy what he has done is arrogant if not downright foolish. The reason he became so wealthy is because he is very good at doing something that is very difficult for most anyone else to do.

Unfortunately, because it serves their own interests, traditional Wall Street has convinced investors that being a Warren Buffett is simple and easy. Wall Street wants us to be long-term buy-and-hold investors for a number of reasons (as discussed in Chapter 5, "Why Conventional Investment Advice Ensures Mediocre Results"). Consequently, they push us to adopt this long-term style of investing that is really nothing more than putting your money in a slot machine and hoping for the best.

The investment approach that we are encouraged to adopt is to come up with a big theory or idea, embrace a stock that embodies it, and then sit and wait for many years for destiny to be fulfilled. You might be one of the lucky few who actually latch on to the right situation in the early stages and make some good money. But for most investors, this long-term, passive approach in which you abandon control of your investment in the hopes that some long-term thesis will play out is a guaranteed way to produce poor returns.

One of the reasons that this approach enjoys so much attention is because we all like to believe we have superior insight into or vision about the future. As we go about our lives, we observe fads, trends, issues, problems, and proposed solutions for the ills of the world. So why not extrapolate from what we see and invest some money in an idea that is likely to prosper if our vision of the world is correct?

Unfortunately, things seldom have a way of working out the way we might think. Just consider the evolution of something like the music business from vinyl records, to eight-track tapes, to cassettes, to CDs, to peer-to-peer sharing, to iPods—and who knows what is next. Even if you do identify a trend, it is extremely difficult to identify a specific stock that will profit from it. When Internet stocks first became a force in the market, the current giant, Google, didn't even exist. If you tried to capture profits in the Internet trend and bought a stock like Yahoo! back in 1999, you would have lost money subsequently.

The idea that we can readily identify big trends and find ways to profit from them is seductive. Millions of people try to do it every day, and most will be wrong. It can be a fun game to play, but as an investment method, it is fraught with peril.

Another reason there is so much support for the idea that long-term buy and hold is the way to become rich is a function of what I call "retroactive genius." In the field of statistics, this is called "data mining" or "data fitting." When you look through historical data, it's easy to cherry-pick a situation that fits the theory you are trying to prove. If you want to prove that the buy-and-hold approach to investing is superior, you simply look back and find the stocks that have per-formed the best over a very long period of time and use those for your example. No one can dispute that if you had actually bought some of these big winners and held on, you would have made a ton of money. If you had bought a big chunk of Starbucks stock when it first went public and held it until today, you would be very rich. No doubt about it. What this sort of data analysis doesn't tell you is how to duplicate that feat in the future.

The next time someone tells you that long-term buy-and-hold is the way to go, simply ask him what he thinks will be the next Cisco or Dell Computers over the next 20 years. His answer might cause you to be a bit uncertain about how easy this is. You have to wonder if anyone is really capable of identifying which stocks are likely to be the stellar performers over the next decade or if it's just luck when it happens. Someone may latch on to a great idea, and in retrospect it will seem obvious, but finding that situation is more likely luck rather than skill. How many times have we heard a company called "the next Microsoft," and what happened to all those promising stocks? For every person who caught the next Microsoft in its very early stages, there are thousands who bought a run-of-the mill, mediocre stock that did little or nothing. In many cases folks did even worse when they loaded up on some hot tip—the next Enron, Worldcom, or some other doomed story. The buy-and-hold approach to investing simply compounds the problem by keeping your money tied up way too long.

Finding the next great stock you can hold for the long run not only is extremely difficult but also is a very risky investing approach. After all, if you want to get in on the ground floor, doesn't that by definition mean buying something that is unproven and unknown and therefore risky? The stocks that turn out to be the biggest winners over time are usually extremely dangerous in their early stages, when the big gains come. In most cases, conservative investors would never have bought them in the first place. It is only when these stocks are mature and have proven themselves for a number of years that they become safe enough to hold for the long term. The irony is that they most likely have already seen their best gains.

Even when you do find a good stock in the early stages, it can be dangerous to your financial well-being to tie up your precious capital, waiting for years for your chosen stock to live up to expectations. If it turns out you made a mistake, not only might you lose money on your investment, but you also will have missed out on all the profits you could have made elsewhere over the years.

One of the stocks that was a great success for Warren Buffet was Coca-Cola. However, if you had waited until ten years ago to buy Coca-Cola, you might not have thought buying and holding was such a fantastic idea. As shown in Figure 4.1, Coca-Cola has done nothing over the past decade.

Chart courtesy of TeleChart® by Worden Brothers, Inc. www.worden.com

FIGURE 4.1   Coca-Cola.

If you have held Coca-Cola stock, you have done even worse than if you had simply parked your cash in an ordinary savings account at your local bank. Even worse, you have taken on much more risk of loss and may even have suffered stress and anxiety as you have worried about the safety of your precious capital.

So what is an investor to do? If you really want the best odds of making money in the market, forget the pipe dream of trying to buy a stock that will go up one-thousand-fold over the course of many years. Instead, learn to invest in stocks that are acting well right now and have the potential to make you money immediately. The more effective and less dangerous way to produce steady investing profits over many years is the Shark Investing method.

Shark Investors don't waste their time and energy on the nearly impossible task of trying to find a couple good stocks they can buy and forget over many years. Shark Investors seize the opportunities in front of them and then waste no time moving on to the next chance to make money. I will discuss exactly how to do this in great detail later, but the key idea is that long-term buy-and-hold investing is like playing the lottery. You place a bet and then simply hope. Shark Investing is like being a professional gambler with an edge. You may have some good luck or bad luck with any given stock, but over the long run you know you will ultimately win, because you maintain control over your destiny.

The Shark Investing approach requires more work and effort, but the benefit is that you greatly reduce risk because you stay in control rather than abandoning your financial well-being to the whims of the long term. Simply holding on to a great stock for years is easy, and it certainly has appeal. Getting rich by doing nothing other than finding a good idea before everyone else is everyone's dream. I'd love to tell you how you can easily do just that, but I'd be lying to you, just like all the brokers and investment advisors who insist this is the only way to invest.

If you really want to compound your investment account quickly, you need to forget that sort of dreaming. Focus instead on finding what is working now and then move on to the next thing that is working. The key is what I call the velocity of your capital. The big money is made by keeping your money fully at work at all times in the best-acting stocks, which generally are smaller, lesser-known stocks. When a position falters, you show little mercy. You move on to another that is showing promise. You want your capital to stay in motion, working hard for you at all times, rather than languishing on a cloud of hope.

Of course, Shark Investing is not easy, but most good things in life require effort. Do you really believe that the way to make big money in the stock market is to come up with a good idea and then do nothing else for decades? Maybe the investing gods will smile on you, but I wouldn't count on it. Shark Investing is the way to have some say in your investing success. It requires vigilance, a steady stream of new ideas, a disciplined approach, perseverance, and, above all, the right mind-set, but the rewards make it worth it.

I'm so passionate about how much better the Shark Investing approach is than the standard buy-and-hold approach that I never miss a chance to make my point. At most social gatherings I attend, the conversation usually turns to investing and the stock market at some point. As a recovering attorney, I always enjoy cross-examining folks over the logic behind their investment approach. Most investors have been so thoroughly brainwashed by the business media and traditional Wall Street "wisdom" that they find some of my Shark Investing view of the market quite surprising. You may want to pursue a discussion like this yourself the next time you have a chance because it provides such great insight into the flawed traditional thinking that so many have embraced.

Here is a typical dialogue:

RevShark: So, tell me about your investing. What is your approach to the stock market?

Investor: I am very conservative. I just buy and hold high-quality blue-chip stocks for the long run.

RevShark: Whoa! You must be a real cowboy to take such a high-risk approach with your money. Do you have any trouble sleeping at night?

Investor: What the heck are you talking about? I don't take big risks. What's risky about holding on to good stocks for a long time?

RevShark: What "good" stocks are you currently holding for the long term?

Investor: General Electric, Dell Computers, Wal-mart, and Coca-Cola.

RevShark: So you feel that those are "safe" stocks you can hold without any worry or concern?

Investor: Sure. Everyone knows those are solid companies that won't disappear. They will be in business forever, so I can hold those stocks for years without losing sleep.

RevShark: So, in your approach to investing, a stock can decline over the course of a decade, like some of those you own, and still be considered a safe or good investment?

Investor: Well, those might be bad examples. Lots of stocks continue to go up over the course of many years. You should just hold on to those.

RevShark: So, which stocks would those be? I'd like to buy them myself. How exactly do you find these stocks that will be big winners over time? Isn't it extremely difficult to find a "good" stock at a very early point in its growth?

Investor: My broker has given me some ideas. There are a couple solar energy stocks in particular that I like. I just have to be very patient until they work.

RevShark: So, what happens if you make a mistake and the solar energy stock that you think is solid ends up suffering due to new technology, poor management, or some other unknown issue? There must be 30 or so solar energy stocks to choose from right now. What if you pick the wrong one? You have tied up capital for many years—maybe even lost money and missed out on returns in other places. Isn't that a very risky thing to do?

Investor: No, no, you're missing the point. You just buy solid stocks that don't have high risk.

RevShark: If it's a safe and solid stock, doesn't that mean that there isn't much risk, and if a stock doesn't have some risk, can it really go up in price substantially? Can you really expect a big safe stock to make big gains like a small risky one?

Investor: Maybe not, but a good stock will continue to go up, and if you just hold on and don't sell, you don't even have to pay taxes. That compounding is really a powerful thing.

RevShark: Yes, it sure is, but doesn't it also work in reverse? If the stock you believe is a big long-term winner turns out to be nothing special, you compound your losses by holding on to it. And do you really end up further ahead when you hold on to a stock simply to avoid taxes? Doesn't there come a time when further appreciation becomes limited, so you would be better off paying the tax on the gain and moving to something else? How much in taxes did the people who didn't sell technology stocks in 2000 end up saving?

Investor: You're saying I should be a hyperactive investor who buys and sells constantly? I don't have time for that.

RevShark: No, you don't need to be that active, but keep in mind that long-term buy and hold is very risky compared to a more active approach. Even if you consider your investments only once a month and use some simple money management rules, it's far less risky than the approach you take now.

Investor: Well, I'll talk to my broker, but I bet he won't agree with you and will think I should just stay fully invested in the stocks I already own.

RevShark: Yes, I bet he will. Good luck.

5

Why Conventional Investment Advice Ensures Mediocre Results

Much of what the typical investor knows and believes about investing in the stock market is just plain wrong. Some of the general concepts such as "Buy low, sell high" and "Buy stocks that are fundamentally cheap" are logically indisputable, but most folks really have no idea how to apply such principles in a manner that will make them money.

The problem lies in the fact that the primary sources of investment information are two groups with priorities and agendas that simply don't align with those of individual investors. We don't receive information that helps us outperform the market because most of the people and entities who claim to provide it aren't even aware of what it is like to be a small, individual investor. In addition, they almost always have other considerations that take priority.

The Financial Media

Many individuals obtain information about the stock market from watching market-oriented television shows such as those on CNBC or by reading financial publications like *Money*, *Forbes*, or the *Wall Street Journal*. Certainly some entertaining and insightful information can be found in these places. But ultimately they are of limited use, because the primary goal of financial media isn't to help you make money, but to obtain and keep viewers, subscribers, and advertisers. The financial media measures success not by providing us with good money-making advice but by giving us advice that attracts attention and eyeballs.

The financial media loves to focus on stories about things such as market gurus who make outrageous predictions or the fact that the indices are at record levels or declined in dramatic fashion. That information doesn't help us make money, but it stirs up emotions and attracts attention. A magazine or television show with a headline that the market will go up 50% next year is certain to catch attention. But this sensationalism is extremely dangerous to the casual investor, because it often motivates us to be less than prudent in our investing decisions. Such advice is more likely to set us up for big losses when we are caught up in swirling emotions and forego having a defensive game plan.

The lack of practical advice for the individual investor from the popular media is largely a function of the fact that most of the folks who give financial advice in the media are either professional money managers or journalists who don't actually own stocks. Most large media organizations preclude their employees who write about the stock market from owning the stocks they discuss. The concerns about conflicts of interest outweigh other considerations.

One glaring omission in mainstream business journalism is successful individual investors. These folks can provide the best advice for other individuals who have similar circumstances, needs, and wants. However, the only time individual investors are featured is when they are being used as an example of seemingly excessive or downright silly actions. There is no serious discussion with successful individual investors about their unique circumstances and about how other individuals might invest to profit the best.

Successful individual investors are generally unknown. The best ones tend to become professional money managers as friends and family see they are doing well and ask them to manage their funds. The individual investor who knocks out good returns year after year for his personal account is not someone we ever see or hear about in the financial media. But that is exactly the person who is best suited to give most of us the best investment advice.

What we end up with in the media is advice from someone who manages billions of dollars and has absolutely no appreciation or understanding of the circumstances of the individual investor. Or we have a journalist who constantly interacts with these people and understands the market only on a theoretical level.

The powers that control the financial media don't really care that advice is so badly skewed toward one limited approach. The big mutual funds, brokers, and institutional Wall Street pay their bills through advertising. The worst part of this situation is that the financial media honestly believe that conventional Wall Street advice is the only game in town. They have no idea that there are ways to approach the market beyond what the big funds and brokers tell us.

Brokers and Financial Advisors

The primary goal of brokers and financial advisors isn't to make you money. Making *you* money doesn't necessarily ensure that *they* will make money. The financial industry makes money by holding on to your financial assets. By doing so, they can take a fee whether or not they help you profit. A mutual fund that loses money profits just as much as one that earns money as long as it holds on to your funds.

Brokers make most of their money not from charging you commissions but by charging you a management fee and using your account assets in various ways in their business endeavors. It is nice if they help make you money and keep you happy, but their financial success depends more on holding on to your assets and using them to generate fees rather than managing them effectively.

An article in the *Wall Street Journal*[1] discussed how highly profitable it is for big brokers to pay low interest rates on the idle cash in your brokerage account while reinvesting the sums elsewhere for their own benefit. In 2006 Merrill Lynch earned about $2 billion from this activity alone, which accounted for about 25% of its profits. Brokers don't need to make you money to make money for themselves. They just need to hold on to your capital.

Because the interests of average individual investors are not aligned with those of their financial advisors, much of the advice we receive is questionable. We are almost always discouraged from actively trading in the short term and are almost always are pushed to hold for the longer term. This is because it is easier for financial advisors to hold on to our funds if we only measure success over the course of many years.

We are unlikely to obtain advice from brokers and financial advisors that will benefit us the most because being empowered and in control of our investments means we won't need these folks as much. If we don't need them to tell us to continually hold on to long-term investments, we probably will move some of our assets from their control. Financial advisors count on the fact that they are selling a market approach that requires us to always be committed to the market one way or another. Because we never sell and raise high levels of cash, we are always tied to the advice of the folks who are keeping us tied to the market.

Like those in the financial media, most advisors really do believe the advice they are giving is the best possible. But they have been so brainwashed by the system that they can't even conceive that there are ways to play the game other than how they have been taught. Wall Street never really ponders what is best for the smaller individual investor.

Another problem with the financial industry is that the best advice and most profitable opportunities are not distributed evenly. The big, powerful customers get the best advice. In his book *Confessions of a Street Addict*, Jim Cramer, a very successful fund manager, discusses how he paid huge commissions to brokers to gain access to knowledgeable analysts and brokers. He could obtain key information before it became widely known to the general public. He states that commissions "determine what you are told, what you will know and how much you can find out. If you do a massive amount of commission business analysts will return your calls, brokers will work for you and you will get plenty of ideas to make money...." [2]

Although this sounds like inside information, it doesn't fall within the formal definition. It is simply well-informed people who have done their own research sharing their valuable information for a price. Yes, these folks probably had access to management and facts that the average person could not readily obtain, but that doesn't make their knowledge illegal insider information.

Big-money players like Cramer have always had the inside track on Wall Street, and they always will. As long as they can pay big bucks in the form of commissions or profitable business, they will skim the cream off the top and obtain valuable information that you and I never will. How can we compete with this? We can't. Therefore, we have to find other ways to approach the market that aren't dependent on knowledge that only a select few might have.

Educational Institutions

You might think that schools can help individual investors find an approach that suits them best. After all, there usually is no financial incentive to push investors to adopt one form of investing over another.

Unfortunately, the truth is that financial education is woeful at best and mostly nonexistent. At the college level, discussion of investing almost never goes beyond how to analyze financial statements and portfolio management as practiced by institutional investors. Little if any discussion occurs about the emotional and psychological aspects of the stock market. Most of the focus is on statistical and mathematical studies.

For many years the primary debate in academic circles wasn't about the best way to succeed at making money in the stock market but whether we should even bother to try. Many academicians believe that the stock market is "efficient" to some degree, which means that all information is instantly reflected in prices. Therefore, no one ever has an edge when it comes to producing better-than-average returns. Anyone who does so is dismissed as an aberration.

Like the financial media, the academic community tends to view things primarily from the standpoint of large institutional investors. The individual investor with smaller amounts of capital is generally dismissed as irrelevant while they ponder the proper allocations and time frames for multibillion-dollar investment funds.

The average investor looking for ways to improve his or her investment returns won't learn how to do that by sitting in a classroom.

Conclusion

The average individual investor won't find much financial advice from traditional sources that will help him or her produce better-than-average returns. There is little motivation to do so and, even worse, no recognition that a problem exists.

If you hope to succeed in the market, you will have to go it alone, like the solitary shark. Although at first it may prove difficult to find your way without the guidance of traditional media and financial advisors, ultimately developing your own unique approach that is free of the shackles of conventional wisdom will prove to be the most rewarding thing you can do for your financial well-being.

Endnotes

1. "How Wall Street 'Sweeps' the Cash," *Wall Street Journal*, January 11, 2007.

2. *Confessions of a Street Addict*, Jim Cramer, Simon & Schuster, 2002, p. 52.

6

The Myths of Wall Street

The cowboy/philosopher/humorist Will Rogers said, "It isn't what we don't know that gives us trouble, it's what we know that ain't so." That is particularly true when it comes to the stock market. It is quite easy to believe things about the market that are just flat-out wrong. The average investor is overwhelmed with sincere and well-meaning advice and wisdom about the markets. But when you carefully evaluate many of the basic beliefs, concepts, and ideas, it becomes obvious that much of them are based on flawed fundamental thinking.

False beliefs about the stock market occur largely because Wall Street doesn't really cater to the average individual investor. As I've mentioned, the interests of advisors and traditional Wall Street simply aren't aligned with those of average individual investors. The problem isn't that they are intentionally deceptive and trying to hurt us. It's just that the investment business has developed over the years in such a way that no one really bothers to question whether certain ideas are applicable to all investors. There is no real appreciation of the unique circumstances of the individual investor, so the myths continue, and the harm is done.

In any endeavor, if the foundation is built on unstable ground, the chances of success are diminished. Thus, it is extremely important that we understand some basic truths about the stock market before we can build an effective Shark Investing style for ourselves. To consistently beat the market, we first have to understand the myths and beliefs that hold back most investors. We have had certain concepts beaten into us so consistently for so long that they become ingrained in our thinking. Only after we question the very foundations of conventional investment thought can we understand the power and simplicity of the Shark Investing strategy.

Chapter 4, "Why Long-Term Buy-and-Hold Investing Is Far Riskier Than Shark Investing," explored the biggest and most dangerous myth of all—the superiority of passive long-term buy-and-hold investing. Like most myths, the theory is compelling, but when it is more carefully evaluated, the problems, illogic, and danger become obvious.

This chapter delves into more of the myths perpetuated by traditional Wall Street. Understanding these common misconceptions will help you better understand why most individual investors are doomed to poor investment returns and what steps you can take to be a better investor.

Myth 1: Buy Low, Sell High

One of the most dangerous and ironic investing myths is the well-known phrase "Buy low, sell high." On the surface that doesn't sound like such a bad idea. Shouldn't we seek out "bargains" when we buy a stock? Unfortunately, whether or not a stock actually is a bargain has little to do with how the current price relates to past prices. In fact, the best bargain may actually be a stock that is trading at its highest price, and the worst bargain may be the one trading at its lowest price.

The problem is that we tend to think about buying stocks in much the same way we buy ordinary products. Usually when we go shopping for things, we want to pay less for that item than what someone else paid. If you buy "cheaper" than everyone else, you can take comfort in finding the ultimate bargain. However, it is a mistake to apply that same logic to the stock market. Stocks aren't like a new pair of pants or a can of soup. Their real worth changes dramatically over time. A stock that someone bought last year for $50 may be a lousy bargain today at half the price. However, if everyone else paid $50 for a stock last year and it can now be bought for $20, it sure feels like we are getting a good deal compared to all those poor suckers who paid much more.

The irony of the stock market is that stocks that are trading at their highest price ever may be the best bargains of all. One of the most difficult things for investors to learn is that sometimes it is safer to buy stocks that are going up and hitting highs rather than stocks that are going down and are at their lows.

One way to appreciate the fact that stocks at their highs are often the best bargains is to consider the stocks that have historically been the biggest winners. It is impossible for a stock to be a big winner unless it has consistently traded at its all-time highs. To profit from a stock that eventually doubles or triples, you have to hold on and not "sell high." Buying low and selling high is a sure way to guarantee that you will not be in the best stocks over the longer term. You will constantly be selling the best stocks that will keep going up over time and replacing them with those that are struggling.

One of the best ways to adjust your thinking about buying strong stocks instead of weak ones is to simply look at the charts of some of the biggest winners in the market in recent decades. Consider Microsoft (MSFT:Nasdaq). You could have bought it on a split-adjusted basis of .09 back in April of 1986. By the end of 1987 you would have tripled your money. So the smart thing to do would be to sell "high"? Take the 300% gain and look for the next play? Of course not. Microsoft traded at or near its "high" continually for many years as it marched to over 50 in the spring of 2000.

"Buy low, sell high" may sound good, but it's a poor way to invest and will prevent you from ever owning the best stocks in the market.

Myth 2: Small, Unknown Stocks Are Only for Reckless Gamblers

Traditional Wall Street prefers big brand-name stocks. It is simpler and easier for big funds and institutions to put money into well-known names; in many cases, big funds simply have no choice. Because they are so big, the only stocks that they can buy without owning too much are the biggest ones in the market. Since they tend to focus on these bigger stocks, they automatically dismiss smaller names as unworthy of consideration.

In addition, most brokers and financial advisers are concerned about being called reckless or making "inappropriate" recommendations. If they put you in big, stable stocks like Procter & Gamble or Coca-Cola, no one can say they are doing something too risky, even though the stocks may ultimately produce very poor returns.

Another reason that Wall Street prefers the big names is that they are the ones that generate huge investment banking fees and commissions from big block sales. Wall Street caters to big investors, and big investors buy only the biggest, most liquid stocks. Most big firms don't even bother to research many of the smaller stocks, because the potential investment banking fees are limited, and big clients can't own them.

The good thing about this Wall Street bias against smaller stocks is that it provides great opportunities for individual investors who can take advantage of the limited amount of research and coverage. The small investor has no edge in buying big stocks that are widely followed and researched. But the individual investor who is willing to do some digging can find some real gems among the smaller names. When we hear the phrase "best of breed" applied to big, dominant stocks and negative comments about small stocks, we should be pleased. This means that there will be more opportunities in the market for those who don't follow that bad advice. Smile when the pundits jabber about how they prefer big, well-known names. They are doing us a favor by keeping the small, hidden gems hidden.

Shark Investors have a preference for smaller stocks. The reason is simple: They move faster and bigger than the more widely followed big stocks, and they are much more likely to be misunderstood and mispriced. Therefore, they offer potentially greater rewards. Of course, with greater rewards come greater risks. But the savvy Shark Investor knows that and uses the stringent money management rules discussed in Chapter 10, "Portfolio Management: The Key to Success," to ensure that she cuts her losers quickly if an investment doesn't work out the way she hopes.

The best value and potential are always found among small-cap stocks. If Warren Buffet were starting out today, he would most likely buy small stocks, because they have the best potential. He is too big now and has so much capital to work with that he has no choice but to buy big companies. The big gains are made by catching relatively unknown stocks that have the potential to multiply in price.

Smaller individual investors have the flexibility to move in and out of these stocks as conditions change. They can limit losses fairly easily because they are fast, flexible, and small and can take profits quickly also.

It doesn't matter what sort of market environment we are in. There will always be at least a few opportunities in smaller stocks that are far better than just about anything you can find in the big boys. Daily moves of 10% or more are an everyday occurrence in small stocks. The key, obviously, is finding the right ones, but there always are some.

Of course, small stocks can cut both ways, because they offer greater potential but also greater risk. Stocks that can move up 20% in a day can also move down 30%. If you play the high-risk, high-return game, you must be sure you have a solid investing methodology. That is the beauty of the Shark Investing approach. It helps you manage risk so that you can be more aggressive in going after the small stocks that have greater potential.

Myth 3: You Can't Time the Market, So You Should Stay Fully Invested at All Times

One large advantage individuals have over big funds and institutions is that they can sit in cash for long periods of time if they want to. Traditional Wall Street doesn't like that. They want you to be fully invested all the time. The very mention of "selling" in the presence of a Wall Street Whale is tantamount to heresy. Furthermore, the media, when faced with weakening market conditions, almost always ask market pundits what stocks investors should be buying, rather than the more appropriate question, "How quickly should investors be moving to cash?" Cash simply is not an option for most of Wall Street.

When the market has been struggling, and investors are thinking about pulling some cash out of their portfolio, they usually are confronted with the comment, "You have to stay in the market, because if you miss the early part of a move, you will miss the big gains and underperform." That is the conventional Wall Street response to folks who are contemplating market timing and may end up transferring assets elsewhere.

One of the other arguments you hear quite often is that if you aren't in the market for the ten best days of the year, your performance will suffer. So because it is impossible to know when those days might come, you should just stay fully invested at all times.

The big flaw in this argument is that it overlooks the impact if you aren't in the market on the ten worst days of the year. Quite often the best days closely follow the worst days. If you miss them both, you aren't hurt at all. In fact, if you missed the ten best days as well as the ten worst days, you would come out ahead, because the worst days are usually more dramatic than the best.

Not being in the market all the time or holding large amounts of cash is a great strategic tool for investors. Sure, you might miss some big upside moves at times, but you also will miss some big downside moves. The most important thing is to manage your investments systematically, protect your capital, and not be afraid to sell when the time is right.

Myth 4: Beating the Indices Should Be Your Primary Focus

The focus of most professional investors is to outperform a certain index. If the S&P 500 is up 5%, they want to make sure they return 6%. If the indices are losing money, investors consider it a victory if they lose less. The focus isn't on making money but on how they perform relative to some benchmark index like the Dow Jones Industrial Average or the S&P 500.

The primary reason for this is that most mutual funds are required to stay heavily invested at all times. Since they can't hold large amounts of cash, their goal is to simply lose less than the market when it is in a downtrend. It's OK to lose money as long as they don't lose as much as the indices.

In a 2004 interview with *Slate* magazine, former Merrill Lynch analyst and Amazon guru Henry Blodget made this twisted concept very clear:

> *"...In a bear market, meanwhile, when most stocks are dropping, long-only investors still have to own something—a mutual fund can't just park its assets in cash. In this case, analysts don't help fund managers by opining that every stock in the sector is going to drop; they help by identifying the stocks that will drop least. In relative rating systems, these stocks deserve 'buy' ratings even though they are going down."*[1]

In other words, mutual funds still consider stocks to be buys even if they think they will drop in price. As long as they end up not losing money as fast as the other guys, they are happy and can even advertise and promote their relative outperformance.

Individual investors don't have to worry about those sorts of competitive pressures. We can focus on making money on an absolute basis. Therefore, we can sell stocks aggressively and hold cash as our best investment alternative at certain times.

Because of Wall Street's focus on relative performance compared to an index, the strategic value of selling and holding cash generally is overlooked. Unfortunately, because most investors have a bias toward holding on to stocks, this tends to lead to problems. When a stock is acting poorly and we contemplate what to do, most of us err on the side of not selling. Psychologically, we have a natural tendency against admitting an error, so we don't sell and then hope things will work out. Not only do we have to battle that issue, but we also have to overcome the Wall Street focus on relative performance, which makes it OK to hold losing stocks as long as they aren't losing as fast as the rest of the market.

The difference in the way relative versus absolute performance is viewed provides great insight into why so many fund managers tend to invest in certain ways that are illogical for individual investors. Institutional investors are content to buy stocks that are languishing or even going down because they can still outperform in that way. Since they aren't worried about losing money, like an individual should be, they tend to stay heavily invested at all times, because that holds the best chance of outperforming. If the market is going up, they have to be heavily long to outperform. If the market is going down, they simply have to be in stocks that aren't falling as fast as the overall market to beat that benchmark.

For individual investors, relative outperformance does not put food on the table. You need absolute performance. It is far more important that, at a minimum, you not lose money rather than beat some index or benchmark. An individual who is down only 25% when the markets are down 35% would be a huge success in the fund world, but he would be in trouble financially if he is trying to pay his bills.

Individual investors should avoid the focus on how they do compared to the indices. Their focus should be solely on their capital and keeping it safe while trying to build it. Beating or not beating the indices is irrelevant. Capital preservation is far more important than market outperformance.

Myth 5: Everyone Has Access to the Same Information

The stock market is not a level playing field, but most individuals invest as if it is. They assume they have the same information as everyone else, so they focus on the facts that are readily available to them and ignore how a stock is actually moving. They don't consider that maybe someone out there knows a lot more than they do and perhaps that might account for why a stock is moving the way it is.

We have all seen a situation in which a stock suddenly starts making big moves up or down, and then a short time later significant news is released that explains why that move took place. Time and again we see a stock trade up sharply, and then news is released that the company is being acquired or has won a big contract. Someone out there always knows more than you do, and you shouldn't assume otherwise.

In 2003, *Business Week* published a cover story on hedge fund manager Steve Cohen, founder of SAC Capital Advisors.[2] Mr. Cohen has consistently been on the list of the biggest earners in the stock market. A big part of his success is due to being able to get an edge by getting information first. A lot of folks think that is unfair. Why should some aggressive guy be able to use his financial power to obtain information that you or I could never obtain on our own?

Perhaps this is unfair or unethical, but the fact is that the flow of valuable information is always "asymmetrical." There is always someone who is more connected, or intelligent, or dishonest, and who gets a jump on the rest of the market. That fact is Exhibit A as to why individual investors can't rely too much on the information that is in the public domain. They also must consider how a stock is moving and assume that someone knows more than they do. The best way to do this is to use charts, as discussed in Chapter 9, "Charts: Navigating the Market Seas."

Although folks such as Mr. Cohen can get a jump on the rest of us, it is hard to keep their actions hidden for long. These folks are working with big money, and they tend to move stocks when they act. Word travels quickly when a big trader is making a big play in a specific stock. Managers such as Mr. Cohen leave tracks on the charts when they act on the informational edge that they have. We might not know specifically what is causing a pickup in trading action, but vigilant investors can benefit from spotting a surge in action.

It is just plain foolish to think that it is an even playing field when it comes to receiving valuable information. There is absolutely no way a small individual investor has superior knowledge about a company. But the good news is that Shark Investors don't need an informational edge. They make up for it by moving fast and being reactive. The stock market is not an even playing field, and rather than complain about that fact, we must use it to our advantage by paying close attention to those Wall Street Whales who do have inside information.

Myth 6: Stock Charts Are Useless Voodoo

The academic world and traditional Wall Street have a strong bias against using technical analysis (TA), which is simply the study of stock charts. The general attitude is that any sort of analysis other than the study of financial fundamentals is a waste of time. Chart readers are usually dismissed as downright delusional when they attempt to use past price patterns to predict future prices.

Chapter 9 discusses charts and their value and use. For now, you should understand three things about them. First, charts are the best way to measure the emotions and psychology in the market. Stocks trade because of what investors are feeling and thinking, not just because of the numbers. Second, charts give us clues as to what the big, better-informed buyers are doing. A billion-dollar fund leaves their footprints on a stock chart when they make a move. Third, stock charts provide a framework in which to manage your investments. They help you cut your losses quickly and hold on to your winners. We'll delve into this much further, but the main thing to keep in mind right now is that when you are advised to ignore stock charts, you are being misled.

Myth 7: You Should Buy What You Know

One myth that many investors find particularly hard to resist is "Buy what you know." The idea was popularized by famed Fidelity Mutual Fund manager Peter Lynch in his book *Beating the Street*. Unfortunately, the concept has been badly corrupted over the years. Many folks fall into the trap of buying a company's stock simply because they are familiar with it and like the product. Typically they fail to understand that good products or services don't necessarily correlate to a good stock. However, they are comforted by the familiar. The fact that they see a product in the stores or in a commercial and can interact with the product gives them comfort. Buying a product and using it or visiting a store or restaurant are usually fun things to do, but it is easy to be misled. It is extremely important that the money management rules I discuss in Chapter 10 be applied scrupulously even though you might feel you have some edge because you are familiar with a product or business. Familiarity can be a dangerous thing.

Myth 8: There Is Only One Right Way to Invest

Most investors spend a tremendous amount of time and energy seeking "the answer." They are convinced that there is one simple and easy approach to the stock market that guarantees riches if they can just find it, understand it, and apply it. Investors constantly seek the holy grail of investing. That is probably part of the reason you are reading this book.

The truth is that there is no easy and simple answer to consistent stock market profits. I believe the Shark Investing approach provides a framework in which your chances of success are much better, but it's still up to you to modify the approach so that you can capitalize on your individual strengths.

Most every stock market professional tends to believe that the way he or she approaches investing is the way everyone should invest. There are lots of ways to conquer the Market Beast. There are folks who focus on determining a stock's value by analyzing balance sheets and income statements, those who study charts, those who focus on macroeconomic trends, those who chase momentum, and so on. They all believe they have the answer.

The truth is that the best approach to the market is highly subjective. The best approach depends primarily on you and your particular strengths and weaknesses. We'll discuss this in detail in Chapter 12, "Developing Your Inner Shark." The important thing to understand now is that when it comes to the stock market, one size does not fit all. What is best for a mutual fund or a giant pension plan is unlikely to be what is best for you. There are lots of ways to play the market game. The great thing about the Shark Investing approach is that it allows you to focus on what you do best.

Conclusion

Shark Investing works because it not only recognizes the illogic contained in the many myths perpetrated by Wall Street but also seeks to capitalize on them. Rather than being enticed to follow the traditional wisdom of "Buy low, sell high" and to ignore unknown small stocks, the astute Shark Investor does just the opposite. The savvy Shark knows that if he wants to beat the market, he has to think differently than the other fish in the sea. Make sure you consider these myths, and compensate for them as you venture into the investing waters.

Endnotes

1. http://www.slate.com/id/2108387/
2. http://www.businessweek.com/magazine/content/03_29/b3842001_mz001.htm

7

Understanding Market Dynamics: Mood Swings, Feelings, and Irrationality

Billions of dollars are made and lost in the stock market each day due to simple human emotions. You might have reams of financial data, a team of insightful analysts, and sophisticated computer programs, but they will prove useless against the feelings and emotions of market participants. If you understand the moods, emotions, and psychology that drive investors, you have the most valuable insight you could possibly possess to make money in the market.

Shark Investors are keenly aware of the human element of the market. They use their insight into mob behavior and psychology to maximize their profits. This chapter explores some of the common themes that arise in the market and how you can benefit by looking at them in a new light.

Many people make the mistake of thinking that what moves the market is financial statements, economic reports, and news. Those things may all have some impact, but ultimately the market is primarily an exercise in psychology. Unfortunately, even the best psychologists have a hard time predicting exactly how someone might behave. Trying to guess what an irrational person might do can be futile. The market illustrates that point quite often with movements that defy explanation.

We often see situations where stocks continue to climb even though almost everyone would agree that it is totally unjustified. This occurs because investors are focusing more on other investors and what they might do rather than any inherent characteristic of the stock or the market itself. That is what makes investing based purely on financial statement numbers a mediocre approach. It misses out on the dramatic moves that develop as emotions become extreme.

Profiting from the stock market is exceedingly difficult to do consistently over a long period of time because the market is irrational and emotional. It moves in a manner that has little appreciation for what we might think is reasonable. When the market goes down, it tends to sink further than seems possible. When it rallies, the moves often last longer than seems logical. If you try to apply common sense and logic to the market, you will end up quite frustrated.

The Market Is Nuts

The simple truth is that the market is not logical or reasonable. It is emotional and unstable. A market is nothing more than a crowd of people that has absolutely no regard for what any one person may think. Our logic may be compelling, our arguments loud and strong, and our oratory worthy of a standing ovation, but the market isn't listening. It marches to its own music no matter how penetrating our insight may be. So, do we knock ourselves out arguing and pleading with the market? Do we watch our portfolios waste away while we stand tall and strong and confident that we are right? Heck no! We give into it because it is bigger and stronger and can persist in its seemingly irrational behavior far longer than we can make our money last.

As you know from attending sporting events or concerts, the normal rules of human behavior do not apply when we are in large groups. If we try to predict what a crowd will do based on the reasonable and logical behavior of a single person in isolation, we will most likely be misled. The shy and soft-spoken fellow who lives next door has the potential to turn into a raving maniac when in an excited crowd. And so it goes with the stock market. You can sit and do cold and hard calculations on valuation levels and the reasonableness of prices, but it is as futile as predicting what a teenager might do at a rock concert. The market is not an exercise in calculus. It is primarily an experiment in crowd psychology. One of the most important observations ever made about the stock market was attributed to the economist John Maynard Keynes: "The market can stay irrational far longer than you can stay solvent."

When forecasting what will happen in the stock market, the most important information to have is a clear understanding of the prevailing mind-set and mood. The stronger the level of prevailing emotions and/or expectations, the more likely the market is to make decisive moves. Greed, fear, love, hate, and worry make for good investing opportunities. When we understand what the market is thinking and feeling, we can invest with more conviction and certainty.

Fear Is the Ultimate Driver

A single human emotion is primarily responsible for the course of the market. That emotion is fear. We either fear that we will lose money, or we fear that we will not make enough. Some folks consider greed to be a fundamental emotion that also drives the market. Greed is really just another form of fear. It is the fear, rightly or wrongly, of not having enough of something. Don't underestimate the fear of not making enough money. It manifests itself differently than the fear of losing money, but it's a potent force that does not evaporate quickly.

Fear is always the primary driving force in the stock market. But like all human emotions, it can rise to extreme levels and then suddenly shift. That is why we must always be ready to move quickly.

The tricky thing about an emotion like fear is that it can drive the market in one direction for a very long time, but as it reaches extreme levels, the likelihood is that the market will reverse. The reason for this is that, when fear is building, it draws in more and more people. Ultimately, when everyone is drawn in and fear is at its highest level, all the buying and selling is done and the market starts to reverse.

Fear is the dominate emotion that we must always consider when contemplating where the market might be headed.

On Mourning and the Market

A useful application of psychological principles to the stock market is to consider major changes in the trend of the market in the context of the emotions that someone goes through when mourning a loss. In other words, what do investors think and feel when a steadily rising market suddenly starts to die?

In 1969, Dr. Elisabeth Kubler-Ross wrote *On Death and Dying*, which set forth the five stages of mourning that individuals go through when confronted with a loss:

1. Denial

2. Anger

3. Bargaining/rationalization

4. Depression

5. Acceptance

When the market undergoes a breakdown, many market participants go through this same series of emotions. At first, when the market shows signs of weakening, widespread denial occurs. Market participants simply ignore the possibility that the status quo could possibly change. When the weakness persists, the feeling shifts to anger. Individuals are mad at themselves for not taking action sooner to prevent losses, and they become mad at those who warned them of the developing problems.

The next phase is where we start making deals with ourselves. "If the market will just hold steady or bounce back a little, I will quit fighting and shift my thinking" is something I have found myself saying to myself on occasion. When that doesn't work and the market continues to do something other than what we hoped, we become depressed and feel hopeless: "I really messed up. Now there's no chance I can make any money."

Next investors try to adapt and come to grips with what is happening, but they wrestle with their reservations. Finally, we accept that the market's character has changed, and we go to work looking for ways to profit from it. When we are in tune with reality again, we are positioned to do what really needs to be done.

The value of this type of thinking about the market is twofold. First, apply it to yourself. If you are angry or depressed about your investing, you probably are going through a grieving process as you try to get back in tune with the market. It is also valuable to apply this thinking about emotional stages to the broader market when it appears to be undergoing change. Are market participants in denial? Are they trying too hard to rationalize the action without accepting it? If you look hard at market action, do you find much evidence that you are undergoing the grieving process as the trend struggles to change?

The Wall of Worry and the Slope of Hope

One of the great ironies of the stock market is that the more people believe it will go in one direction, the more likely it is to do the opposite. When everyone thinks it will go down further and that it is a mistake to do any buying, the market has a tendency to go up instead.

This occurs because when investors are worried about the market, they do some selling to prevent losses, which increases their cash reserves.

The more worry there is, the more stocks are sold and the more cash builds up. At some point, the sellers exhaust themselves, and the market stops declining as the selling pressure is relieved. Because most of the selling has been done, it takes just a bit of buying for the market to start inching back up. But all those folks who have been concerned and have been selling tend to stay that way for a while. They don't trust the move back up, and they don't rush back in. That sets the stage for the phenomenon known as "climbing the wall of worry."

The market often has a tendency to climb back up when everyone is worried, because investors have already acted on their worry and sold their stocks. There is no more selling pressure left to force the market down. As the market stops going down and starts to inch back up, these worried folks often decide that they will do a little buying, and this drives the market up a little. Before you know it, the market is slowly and steadily climbing back up as still-worried investors continue to put money to work because they are starting to fear they will be left behind.

This phenomenon also works in reverse. When everyone is hopeful that the market will go up and has used up all their buying power, there is a tendency to "slide down the slope of hope." As stocks fall because there is so little cash left to drive them up, investors start to give up a little bit. They do some selling that pushes stocks down further, which causes more selling, and so on. All the way down the lingering hope that more upside is coming keeps the slide going.

Fear of a Crash

In my early days of trading, one of my biggest mistakes was constantly worrying about a 1987-type crash. Fear that I would be caught in a sudden meltdown of giant proportions with no chance of escape was always in the back of my mind. At certain times when feeling particularly paranoid, I would dump good positions just to protect myself from the crash I was dreaming about at night.

One day, while on the verge of dumping positions again, based on fuzzy fears of a crash, I spent some time studying what had happened in the past. It became quite clear that I had lost far more money worrying about the big one-day crash than I ever would have lost in an actual crash. Giving in to my thoughtless caution and taking myself out of good positions was hurting my returns.

When I went back and studied some of the big crashes, particularly the 1987 meltdown, it was fairly clear that generally there were plenty of warning signs before a crash actually occurred. I was prone to exercise my fits of caution at times when the market had been very strong, which turned out not to be the time when crashes tended to occur. Historically, crashes didn't occur when the market was close to a top and very strong. They came after a period of struggle and some poor action.

If I simply became more cautious only after the market had showed some marked weakness, it was very unlikely I would ever be caught in a crash unless it was caused by some outside event like 9/11. Of course, you don't need a giant crash to hurt your performance; even a mild pullback can inflict a hefty dose of pain. However, selling because of niggling fears about a one-day crash is likely to be a major mistake. Be cautious, but make sure your fears are based on facts and not some murky concerns about crashes.

Fear of Being Left Behind

The fear of being left out when the market is rallying can cause some particularly dramatic action. The market bubble that finally topped out early in 2000 is a classic example. When investors fear being left behind, they chase stocks or markets that are going straight up and/or buy minor pullbacks or dips. This is the reason that the market can become tremendously extended and still have only minor corrections. What is most interesting about the market when it's in this mood is that the ordinary fears of losing money are suppressed. There is often outright denial of the risks that can occur. When this situation occurs, it can produce tremendous profits, but it is exceedingly important to maintain your objectivity and appreciate what is actually happening. A graceful exit is all you need to separate yourself from those who let a substantial profit slip away.

Investors tend to get in trouble when they start thinking the market might be different this time and that it will keep on going for this or that reason. It is never different. The market always has and always will have cycles of ups and downs. There will be times when things go absolutely nuts as people panic and worry that they will miss the opportunity to get rich. When that happens, it can create some exceptional opportunities, but you have to maintain your objectivity and realize that the cyclical nature of the market will eventually kick in.

It Ain't All Brains

Brains are an overrated attribute on Wall Street. You probably know some very smart people who are terrible investors. This often occurs because they are constantly trying to outthink the market. Smart people tend to think logically and have a hard time dealing with a market that ignores what should be painfully obvious. The market is very emotional and illogical at times, and if you are too analytical, you will be surprised often. Using logic to argue with a lunatic is useless, and using logic to figure what the market might do on any given day is equally useless.

Another interesting aspect of "intelligence" on Wall Street is how the negative case for the market almost always has more intellectual appeal than the bull case. In good markets and bad, the bears always sound much more logical and astute than the bulls. Bears always seem to have great intellectual gravitas and profound insight as they talk about how core inflation numbers are misleading, inverted yield curves will lead to recession, variable-rate mortgages will lead to a slump in consumer spending, and things of that sort. You can always find a bear who can make such a compelling case for a horrible market that you can't help but cringe.

Perhaps bears usually sound compelling because cynicism is something we generally associate with experience. Their arguments and logic are always good, but there is one big problem: Markets are not logical; they are emotional. A market moves not because someone punched in numbers and decided it was time to buy or sell. It moves because emotions are strong and it "feels" necessary. Some are acting out of fear and some out of greed, and it doesn't much matter what the bears have to say about anything.

Rookies are never cynics. It's always the grizzled old veteran who has seen it all who tends to be the voice of skepticism. Bulls often sound ignorant or just downright goofy as they dismiss all the negatives that can be found in the headlines every day. Don't be fooled into thinking the only intellectual market position is a negative one. It will always feel that way, but there are times to embrace the Pollyannas of the world.

It is particularly interesting how many longtime market pros seem to become permanent bears over the years. The longer they are in the market, the less seldom they seem to take a bullish view. I suspect that this is largely caused by an increased focus on preserving capital that has been built up over many years. These people want to hang on to what they have and aren't interested in taking risks. Forget the various sentiment indicators, and just look at the headlines. When the media are downcast, the average investor would probably feel downright foolish being optimistic.

The Good News About Bad News

Market participants often overstate the importance of news events. The media often use the news as a fast and easy explanation for what the market is doing, when the real reasons are much more difficult to pin down. One of the more confounding things about the market is how it sometimes seems to have irrational reactions to important news events. The market most often moves because of emotions of participants who have little to do with news. The same news item on different days can generate tremendously different results, depending on investors' moods.

If the market is predisposed to be bullish, it tends to find a way to view what seems to be negative news as positive. We hear arguments such as "It is already priced in" or that some small component of the news is of particular significance. When the bulls are happy and optimistic, they can explain away bad news in the blink of an eye. On other days, when expectations are high and profit-taking is the mindset, no news is good news. Random events have far less impact when mood and sentiment are at extreme levels.

Conclusion

One of the key advantages of Shark Investing is that it recognizes that the stock market is irrational and moody and prone to doing unexpected things. We recognize that we can take steps to profit when the mood is unusually good or run and hide when things become dark and gloomy. We not only want to appreciate the irrationality of the market; we want to embrace it so that we can profit from it. Key to Shark Investing is developing strategies to do just that, as discussed in the next chapter.

Part III

Becoming a
Shark Investor

8

Implementing the Shark Investing Style

Now that we have explored the theory and logic behind Shark Investing and why it is the best approach for individual investors, it is time to find the best way to use these concepts and insights to develop your own investing approach. That means developing some specific guidelines and rules that will help build the foundation of your new investing style and allow you to evolve as things become more comfortable and familiar.

In general, I am not a big fan of following a rule book when it comes to the market. Either the rules change as the market evolves, or the rules are so general that they don't take into account the numerous exceptions that tend to occur. However, some basic things about Shark Investing will never change, and they must become the core of whatever style you choose if you are to be a true Shark Investor.

Shark Investing is like most other worthwhile things in life. If it were extremely easy to learn and do well, it wouldn't be so potentially lucrative. Shark Investing isn't terribly complex or hard to understand, but it requires emotional and intellectual rigor. You will often be tempted to venture off-track, but if you are to prosper over the long run, you will come back to the core values of Shark Investing. It takes some drive, persistence, and effort to implement the Shark Investing style, but if you learn to do it, the time and energy you have expended will be one of the best investments you can make.

As we discussed in Chapter 3, "What Is Shark Investing?" Shark Investing is about moving fast, aggressively, and opportunistically while staying risk-averse. You have to admit the theory sure sounds like it should produce good results, but how do you implement the thinking? The following sections discuss my Ten Commandments of Shark Investing that help lay the foundation. We'll discuss these concepts in much greater detail, but at this point it is important to understand the reasons behind the commandments, how they influence our actions, and how they fit together.

Let's review the nine key attributes of the Investing Shark that we discussed in Chapter 3:

- Sharks are aggressive. When the time is right, we attack, and we don't linger when conditions change.

- Sharks are opportunistic and reactive. We capitalize on what is happening right now and are not overly anticipatory.

- Sharks stay in motion. We don't sit around and hope. We keep looking for opportunities.

- Sharks plan their attacks. We always know what we are going to do as stocks move up and down.

- Sharks are patient while they stalk their prey. We don't act rashly. We watch for opportunities to develop, act decisively, and have no qualms about moving on.

- Sharks take advantage of the emotions of the crowd as it becomes frenzied and emotional. The crowd makes for a good meal.

- Sharks don't have emotional or sentimental attachments to the stocks they profit from. Use 'em and lose 'em is our motto. There is always another opportunity around the corner.

- Sharks are risk-averse and do not hesitate to swim away the moment they sense danger. The sea gives us an endless bounty as long as we have capital to invest.

- Sharks have an attitude. We are fast, aggressive, and masters of our investing fate.

Make sure you understand the thinking and reasons behind these characteristics and why they help make you a better investor. Contemplate how you might amend your current approach to the market to be more consistent with the Shark Investing principles. The next step is to turn theory into action.

The Ten Commandments of Shark Investing

Now that you know how the successful Investing Shark thinks, you need to make sure your behavior conforms. The following sections describe the ten basic rules of the successful Shark.

1. Thou Shalt Protect Thy Capital

The most important commandment is the first one. Capital keeps you in the investing game. As long as you have funds to work with, the potential for success exists. If you focus on maintaining your capital base, the potential for victory is always there.

2. Thou Shalt Use a Money Management System Without Fail

Money management is the cornerstone of Shark Investing. You can be a mediocre stock picker, but if you are effective at managing your stocks after you buy them, you can still produce excellent results. All money management systems are built around one key consideration: not letting losses grow too big. Everything else is secondary. Making up losses requires substantial work. You must avoid digging yourself into a hole, because it so costly and demoralizing to work your way out of it. The great thing about the market is that new opportunities arise every day. If you protect your capital, you will never run out of chances to produce stellar returns.

Your goal as a Shark Investor is to develop a system that not only methodically cuts losses quickly but also locks in profits as your investments succeed. You need to have a plan. Anyone can throw money at the stock market, and quite often they will experience some good luck, but over the long run, success comes from applying a systematic approach. It might be fundamental, technical, or even astrological, but you need a plan of attack to conquer the market beast. Luck will take you only so far, and eventually it will cost you.

3. Thou Shalt Use Charts

Charts provide a logical and systematic framework in which to implement a money management system. They help remove emotion from deciding when to take a loss or lock in a profit. Charts also serve as a predictive tool that help you understand the emotions that are driving prices, and they give you insight into where things might be headed.

4. Thou Shalt Diversify Not Only by Security but Also by Price and Time Frame

If you invest in the stock market, you have to become used to the fact that you will be wrong a lot and will be surprised by negative news quite often. There will be times when you buy at the high price and sell at the low price, no matter how hard you work or how smart you might be. Bad investments are going to happen. The important thing is that you avoid compounding your errors, and you do that by diversifying. My mantra is "partial buys, partial sells." I know I won't always buy or sell at the best price, but if I average in and out of my positions with several buys or sells, I tend to smooth out my errors. I'll divide my position so that I might take a quick profit or loss on a portion and give another portion more room to run.

5. Thou Shalt Act Aggressively When the Odds Are in Thy Favor

If you want to make money in the market, you can't be too timid or overly cautious. When opportunities begin to arise, you need to act aggressively to take advantage of them. If you are too risk-averse, you will always be left on the sidelines. At some point you must stop planning and take action.

It is often quite difficult to shift from a cautious, risk-averse position to a highly aggressive profit-seeking one. You will often have to consciously push yourself to do this, and it can feel quite uncomfortable. It takes practice and experience, but once you become accustomed to making these quick strategic shifts, it becomes easier and you will realize how powerful a tool being highly aggressive is.

The advantage that individual investors have is that because we are small, we can be extremely fast. Quickness gives us a huge advantage over the lumbering elephantine funds and big-time investors who are trying to put billions of dollars to work. We can sell and rebuy in the blink of an eye and not create a ripple. Thus, it is to our advantage to be aggressive when the time is right, because we can always reverse course. It is easy to always be cautious, so you need to consciously overcome that and remember that being small has its advantages.

Consider two investors of roughly equal ability—one with an account of $150,000, and the other with an account of $150 million. Who will produce a better percentage return? My money is on the investor with the smaller account. Why? She can focus on a small number of stocks, can move fast and get out and in with a minimum of slippage, and doesn't get trapped because of a lack of liquidity. When a stock perks up, she acts aggressively and buys immediately. When a stock rolls over, she is out the door in a flash.

Because of the great quickness advantage we have as small investors, it's much easier to be reactive to news and market events rather than anticipatory. We do not have to position ourselves in advance. I don't know what this market will do tomorrow, but I don't have to worry about it too much, because I have speed on my side. A small investor is a jaguar in a world of elephants. Don't squander your ability to be aggressive. Use it.

6. Thou Shalt Not Be Afraid to Sell

Selling is the most overlooked strategic tool in investing. It is easy to do, easy to undo, and extremely powerful. Traditional Wall Street has a strong bias against selling and actively discourages it. Shark investors ignore that advice.

7. Thou Shalt Respect the Illogic of the Market and the Role of Luck

The stock market is an irrational beast. No matter what you do, it will treat you badly at times and unjustly reward you at other times. You always have to be ready for unfair treatment and make sure you take steps so that bad luck doesn't hurt you so much that it uses up your capital. When you have good luck, you have to make sure you take advantage and not let it slip away.

8. Thou Shalt Not Invest as if You Are Managing a Fund, Unless You Are a Fund Manager

Too many investors handicap themselves by thinking and acting as if they are miniature mutual funds. What they forget is that nimble individual investors have a huge advantage over big lumbering funds. They can move extremely fast. If you have a plan, you can go from 100% cash to fully invested in the blink of an eye. Big funds have to position themselves gradually and try to anticipate. Individuals can afford to be more patient and can be more reactive to the market when it is safer.

Also, fund managers are judged based on how they perform versus a benchmark index. Whether they actually make money is a secondary consideration. In the world of funds, if you lose less money than your benchmark index, you are considered a success. Don't get pulled into that mind-set. Forget the indices, and focus on producing real profits. The primary impact of this sort of thinking is that you will focus more on accurate timing and will have far less tolerance for riding stocks down. You should have no fear of holding high cash balances when the market is struggling. Fund managers are happy to be fully invested in a downtrending market if they aren't losing money any faster than their benchmark index. Individual investors should cringe at that thought. When you are losing money at a slower rate than the market, you are still digging a hole that will take a lot of work to fill.

9. Thou Shalt Be Patient, Persistent, and Methodical

Your mental state makes a huge difference in how you look at the market. You have to control your frustration and euphoria. Don't get too down on yourself when you are having a hard time, and don't get too excited when you have success. An even temperament is a valuable quality for investors. If you recognize that you will have good luck and bad luck, and you keep plugging along, success is likely to be yours.

Do you have to be a genius to be a great investor? No. What you do need is the ability to understand and control your emotions. Balancing fear, greed, panic, and euphoria, along with some common sense and a decent methodology, will go a long way toward making you a successful trader. Investing isn't rocket science. It can be pretty simple at times, but it's easy to mess it up with your emotions.

Stay mentally and physically healthy. Trading is hard work. If you aren't feeling well physically and mentally, the market will be able to beat you. You need to be alert, strong, and mentally and emotionally focused to be at the top of your game.

Don't give up. This can be a tough business for long stretches of time, but the payoffs are tremendous when they come. The great thing about the market is that it produces a new crop of opportunities day after day. If you don't give up and just keep plodding along, you can take comfort in the fact that you will have another chance to make money very soon. It is only when you let the market convince you that it is impossible to make money that you are defeated.

10. Thou Shalt Never Stop Educating Thyself

One of the reasons that the market is so fascinating is that it combines elements of psychology, business, mathematics, and numerous other disciplines and sciences. There are always new approaches and theories about the best way to handle the market. The more you read about and study the market, the more insight you will have into the dynamics that affect it. Constant education helps you stay on the cutting edge. Emotions can be our worst enemy. If we are heavily long, we tend to seek out bullish evidence to support that bias. We need to be conscious of our inclination to be swayed by our positions. Absolute objectivity is probably impossible, but we need to strive for it nonetheless.

It's easy to get stuck in how you usually think and evaluate things. When you break the thought patterns that are safe, secure, and reflexive, that is when you reach a higher intellectual plane. Mind-set is so important to a trader. You have to be very aware of your thought patterns and the traps you fall into. How do you think about your trading and the market? Are you stuck in certain thought patterns that prevent you from progressing as a trader? I'm quite often surprised by the comments I receive in the mail that are so full of absolutes and certainties. Traders have to consider various scenarios and strategies, but you have to think outside the box as well.

The best investors develop their own style that takes into account their particular strengths, weaknesses, and personality quirks. Don't try to mimic someone else, but keep in mind that you can learn from everyone. Take bits and pieces of various methods, and develop something that is comfortable for you.

Tools of the Shark

Now that we have the rules, let's get to the tools. This is what you need:

- A computer with Internet access. You must be able to access charts and brokers and do research. All the information you need is readily and easily accessible on the Internet.

- An online brokerage account. There are many good online brokers, such as Etrade.com, Schwab.com, and TDAmeritrade.com. There are lots of relatively minor differences, but for the most part they are fast, cheap, and reliable.

- Charts. A number of good charting programs are available for free or at low cost on the Internet, such as at BigCharts.com and StockCharts.com. My favorite is Telechart, which is available for a fee at Telechart.com.

- News and fundamental data. Either Yahoo! Finance or Google Finance will provide you with all the fundamental data and news that you need, and they are free.

- Ideas. Now that you are all set up, you need some good ideas to put the Shark method to the test. One good place to start is *Investors Business Daily*. It has numerous lists of interesting stocks and tends to be oriented toward the individual investor. Many websites provide you with ideas and advice, such as theStreet.com and the website I operate, SharkInvesting.com. It is easy to be overwhelmed by ideas, so you need to learn to be selective. As you develop your Shark Investing style, the best sources of ideas will become clearer.

That is all you need to start becoming a successful Investing Shark. Now let's put those tools to work.

9

Charts: Navigating the Market Seas

Charts are a Shark Investor's most valuable tool. They help us identify good investments, form the basis of our battle plans, and let us know when it is time to aggressively attack and when it is time to run for the safety of cash. Charts help create order in the chaos that is the market and give us clear information on which to act.

Ultimately, when it comes to determining whether you are a successful investor, the only thing that matters is the price at which you buy and sell the stocks you invest in. All the news, debates, and discussions that fill the media are irrelevant in the end, because price is always the final arbiter. Charts keep the focus on the only thing that really matters and free us from the endless and unwinnable debates over valuation, fundamentals, and economics.

Charts serve two primary purposes for the Shark Investor. The first, which we will discuss in this chapter, is that they are predictive tools. They help us determine what a stock might do in the future. Charts certainly are not infallible in that regard, but they help us see the patterns and emotions that are driving prices and provide insight into how the future might unfold.

The second purpose of charts, which we will discuss in the next chapter, is that they provide a framework in which we can set up an effective structure in which to manage our investments. The key to producing exceptional returns is to make sure we minimize losses and maximize gains. Charts are the ideal tool for setting up a system of rules in which to do that.

Traditional Wall Street will tell you that charts are nonsense. The argument is that past price activity has no impact on future price action. Go ahead and draw a bunch of lines and patterns, but all that really matters are the fundamentals. If a stock is a good value, it doesn't much matter what the price might have been. We are fooling ourselves if we think we gain any added insight by studying the history of a stock's price and volume.

As discussed in prior chapters, traditional Wall Street has a strong preference for fundamental analysis. What money managers, funds, and brokers have to sell is their superior research. If they admit that chart reading has validity, it tends to undermine what they are selling us, because anyone can look at a chart and try to draw conclusions. If Wall Street professionals admit that chart reading is a valuable tool, what do we need Wall Street professionals for?

Those who understand the role of chart reading, also called technical analysis (TA), point out that it is basically the study of psychology. Its value lies in its ability to help you understand the psychological shifts and behavioral trends in individual stocks as well as the broad market. People have fairly predictable emotional responses as stocks become cheaper or more expensive and their profits, losses, and available entry points change. If you understand investors' past behavior, you can predict their future behavior.

If you want proof that past prices affect how a stock acts, consider how you feel and act when you hold a stock in which you have a big gain that is trading at its all-time highs. Compare this to a stock in which you have a big loss that is dragging along at its lowest price in years. Is it likely that you might think, feel, and act differently in these two different situations? If you say yes, you can be pretty confident that you are not alone.

Think of chart reading as a soft science or even an art rather than a set of hard-and-fast rules that must always be applied in the same way. Stocks are just like people, because that is who makes them look the way they do, by buying and selling as emotions ebb and flow. Just like people, stocks can be unpredictable, but certain emotions and behaviors do occur regularly.

Most of the detractors of technical analysis make the mistake of characterizing chart reading as a science with a never-changing set of rules. They like to think that chart reading is just some robotic application of a rule book that can't be shown to have any statistical support. They are missing the fact that charts are a graphical depiction of psychology.

One hard-core-value investor and detractor of charts commented that "You won't find a chartist on the Forbes 400 list of America's richest people, and that's probably because charting is inherently backward-looking.... Investment fortune requires a forward-looking approach.... Charts don't give you that; they only give you a great picture of where the market has been."

First, let's dismiss the idea that the way to determine the effectiveness of chart reading is to look at how many chart readers are on the Forbes 400 list. Even if the implication that you can't become a billionaire by using charts for investing was correct, you can still make millions of dollars using them as investing tools. I know because I have done it myself and know other people who have, also.

In any event, the Forbes list does indeed include a number of investors who use chart reading. George Soros, for one, has written that "Technical analysis studies market patterns and the demand and supply of stocks. It has undoubted merit in predicting probabilities." How about John W. Henry, the owner of the Boston Red Sox? He used a form of TA known as "trend following" and increased a trading account from $16,000 to over $1 billion.

There is no question that size does have a major impact on investment methods: The more money you are investing, the more difficult it becomes to use charts effectively. Someone with hundreds of millions of dollars to invest can't invest like an individual with $10,000. A giant fund with huge sums to put to work can't react to chart patterns like you or me. These Whales actually create the chart as they make their moves.

This leads to another valuable aspect of using charts. A chart allows us to follow the elephant tracks of major market participants such as mutual funds and those who are in the Forbes 400. These folks can't buy a stock without it being reflected in the chart, and the flexible and fast-moving Shark Investor can follow along for the ride. At some point, if you make enough money your problem becomes that you can't make moves without impacting the charts. When that time comes, you will then have to deal with the problems of being a successful investing Whale. In the meantime, you can use charts to piggyback what the big boys are doing. Is chart reading backward-looking and therefore ineffective? Unless you are psychic, all investing, both technical and fundamental, is nothing more than trying to predict the future by looking at past events. Technical investors consider the past price action of a stock, whereas fundamental investors study past financial results. Both then try to use that information to predict how the future will unfold.

Are past fundamentals a better predictor of future stock action than a stock's past price action? The academics can argue over that point, but I think we can safely conclude it depends on the individual investor. Some will do better with charts and some will do better with fundamentals. Time frames, investing style, and the personal characteristics of the investor will affect that answer. At the end of the day, the only thing that matters when making decisions about a stock is whether we are losing money or making money—and that is what a chart is all about. Using a chart to make decisions ensures that you are always guarding your precious capital.

The Misuse of Charts

The biggest problem with chart reading is that much of it is really bad— even nonsensical. Name a way to look at a chart, and I guarantee it's been done. From astrology to chaos theory, charts have been sliced, diced, and pureed in hopes of finding "The Secret" that will unlock rivers of profits. Having some sort of structure with which to approach the market is helpful, but people go far beyond that and spend many millions of dollars each year trying to find infallible mechanical trading systems. If it were easy to design such things, the big money on Wall Street would simply hire all the best programmers and make money all day.

The search for the technical holy grail has gone on as long as the market has existed, and there have been systems that work for periods of time. Back-testing to see if certain patterns hold some special magic is a major industry. All sorts of programs are available that claim to have developed algorithms that will make you rich if you just follow the red and green signals. Some big hedge funds have developed complex "black box" systems that are used to trade the market. One of the most famous and most secretive is run by Ed Thorp. Prior to turning his efforts to Wall Street, Thorp was a well-known professional gambler who wrote one of the first books about card counting and basic blackjack strategy. These "black box" mechanical trading systems used by folks like Thorp require constant modifications and updates because what works changes so often.

Mechanical trading systems based on charts can work, but few of them are adaptable to the ever-changing market environment. A system that uses a momentum scheme will break down in a trading-range market, and a system that focuses on overbought conditions will underperform in a strong trending market. Despite all our efforts to quantify and understand the market, it will always be random and unpredictable to some extent. It simply is not possible to predict the news or how people will react to it. Some things remain constant, but not to the degree that we can ever be confident that we can capture the swings in the market through the use of a couple of simple indicators.

Chart Basics

A chart is nothing more than a graphical depiction of a stock's price history over a certain period of time. Just about any time frame can be used, from several decades to mere minutes. In addition to price, volume is typically shown on a chart as well, because it is often useful to know if a stock's price movement is a product of more buying and selling than is typical. If a stock moves up on high volume, that may have a different meaning than if it moved on below-average volume.

The three basic types of charts are line charts, bar charts, and Japanese candlestick charts.

A line chart, shown in Figure 9.1, has a line that connects each day's closing price to each other.

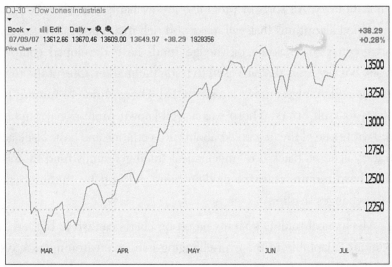

Chart courtesy of TeleChart® by Worden Brothers, Inc. www.worden.com

FIGURE 9.1   A line chart.

A bar chart, shown in Figure 9.2, adds information and shows the closing and opening prices each day. If you use a shorter time frame for your investing, that can be an important consideration.

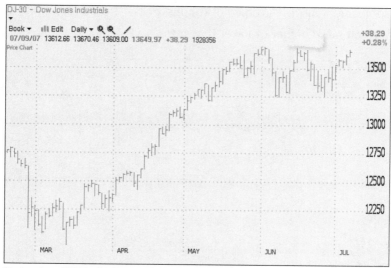

Chart courtesy of TeleChart® by Worden Brothers, Inc. www.worden.com

FIGURE 9.2   A bar chart.

The third type of chart, which is what I use, is called a Japanese candlestick chart (see Figure 9.3). This form of chart was first used by rice traders in Japan many centuries ago. Candlestick charts make it easy to see if a stock has closed up or down on a particular day. If the "candlestick" is colored, the stock closed lower than it opened. If the "candlestick" is white or open, the stock closed higher than it opened. The "wick" shows if the stock traded above or below the opening and closing prices of the day.

If you are so inclined, you can add much more information to your charts. The information that is added is referred to as "'indicators" and is derived from the price and volume action. It is an attempt to summarize and clarify what is there. For example, you might add a moving average indicator. This is just a line that shows what a stock's average price has been over a set period of time. The 50-day moving average is commonly used. It changes each day as the first of the last 50 days is dropped and the current day is added. Figure 9.4 shows what the 50-day moving average looks like on a candlestick chart of Dell Computers. I added

volume and a moving average of volume so that I can more easily see
if the volume is higher or lower than average.

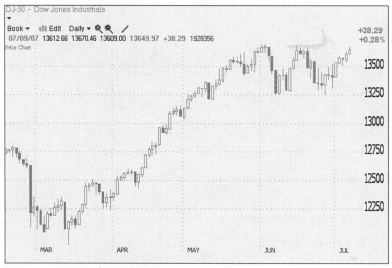

Chart courtesy of TeleChart® by Worden Brothers, Inc. www.worden.com

FIGURE 9.3   A Japanese candlestick chart.

Chart courtesy of TeleChart® by Worden Brothers, Inc. www.worden.com

FIGURE 9.4   The 50-day moving average on a candlestick chart.

All that a moving average does is summarize the price data and makes it easier to see which way the stock is moving and how fast it has been moving up. As you can see from Figure 9.4, the stock had been trending up for a while but lost some of its momentum and traded down to the 50-day moving average. When a stock's momentum slows like this, it may be a good time to consider a sale.

Of course, you don't need the 50-day moving average to tell you that the price has been slipping recently, because this is readily apparently from the price. However, it can be helpful to see the price summarized in this manner, by an indicator like a moving average.

In addition to moving averages, many other indicators can be added to your charts. A few of the more common include stochastics, MACD, Bollinger bands, RSI, ADX, Fibonacci fans, and linear regression. All that any of these indicators do is attempt to manipulate and summarize the data to make it easier for you to see a characteristic you might find useful. Some people find that valuable, and others don't.

Personally, I do not find most indicators to be of any great value. The only ones that I use are moving averages of price over periods of 50 and 200 days. These lines give me a quick and convenient gauge of how strong a stock has been. If a stock suddenly starts to trade under its 50-day moving average after being above that level for some time, I know that it is undergoing considerable weakening.

Figure 9.5 shows a typical chart I use.

So what do we do with these charts? How are they useful? It is nice to know where a stock has been in the past, but does that help us determine where the stock might go in the future? Charts help us understand the emotions, psychology, and behavior that ultimately move stocks as well as the entire market. Because charts track the feelings and thinking of market participants, they provide insight into future price movements.

Obviously, if we could predict with complete certainty how a stock will act in the future, we'd all be having tea with some guy wearing a monocle on our yachts. We can never be 100% confident about what a stock will do. The goal of chart readers is to become as confident as humanly possible. Keep in mind that technical analysis is primarily an exercise in psychology, not math.

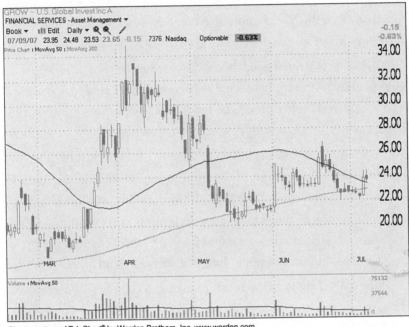

Chart courtesy of TeleChart® by Worden Brothers, Inc. www.worden.com

FIGURE 9.5   A typical chart I use.

Chart reading is based on one basic concept: As a stock moves up and down, and people enjoy gains or suffer losses, they have an emotional reaction that may drive them to take certain actions. There is absolutely no doubt in my mind that TA is valid, for two reasons. First, it has too many followers to not be self-fulfilling to some degree. Second, if you believe that people have similar emotional reactions as their stocks make or lose them money, it is capable of measurement, which is what TA is all about.

Let's consider an example. Mary and her husband Gary dabble in the stock market with mixed success. Recently Mary had coffee with a friend who had just returned from a trip to China. Mary was surprised when her friend told her that she had enjoyed a venti cafe latte at a Starbucks while in Beijing.

Later that day, as Mary was pondering what to do with her recent company bonus, she recalled the conversation and thought she would look into Starbucks further. It certainly was a solid company. Even though it seems to be everywhere in the United States, maybe it has good potential if it is starting to expand into countries like China.

Mary checks her online brokerage account and sees that the stock is trading around 34. The chart looks like Figure 9.6.

Chart courtesy of TeleChart® by Worden Brothers, Inc. www.worden.com

FIGURE 9.6   Starbucks trading around 34.

The next day Mary signs on to her account again and sees that Starbucks is trading up sharply after reporting that sales were quite good in the prior month. She decides to jump in anyway and buys 300 shares at $35.50. Later that night she is quite pleased when she sees the stock closed at almost $36.

The next day Starbucks announces that it plans to open 2,400 new stores around the world and sees revenues growing 20%. The stock leaps higher, and Mary now has a gain of around $1,000. She is quite pleased with her investing prowess and quickly dismisses her husband's advice to "take the money and run." She is obviously on to something with the idea of global expansion, and it is sure to be in its early stages. This is a great stock that she plans to hold on to for the long term as it moves steadily higher.

Over the next few weeks the stock pulls back slightly, and Mary is a bit upset that she didn't take the quick profit that her know-it-all husband suggested. She makes a mental note that the next time the stock is close to $40, she will take some profits so she can do a little shopping. Several weeks later the stock starts to climb again and actually hits $40 during the course of the day (see Figure 9.7). Mary plans to sell the next day, but before she can do so, an analyst downgrades the stock, and it trades down $2.

Chart courtesy of TeleChart® by Worden Brothers, Inc. www.worden.com

FIGURE 9.7   The stock starts to climb again.

Mary is unhappy that she missed two good chances to sell some shares for a good profit. She won't let that happen again. She still has a good gain but is mad at herself that she let it slip. She continues to watch the stock. Not only does it not bounce back, but it keeps drifting down. It jumps up slightly for a couple days but then proceeds to drift lower again (see Figure 9.8). Several weeks later Mary is sitting on a loss of a couple hundred dollars instead of the hefty $1,000 profit she had a couple months ago.

Chart courtesy of TeleChart® by Worden Brothers, Inc. www.worden.com

FIGURE 9.8   The stock keeps drifting down.

Mary is just one of many people who share common emotions as a stock they own goes through gyrations. Thousands of others bought shares and missed the opportunity to take substantial profits as the stock approached 40. What is the likely behavior of those people if and when the stock moves back toward 40? Many will be inclined to sell and take the profits that they regret not taking early.

What happens if the stock continues to trend down for a while and many of the holders see their unrealized profits turn into losses? Many of them will look for opportunities to sell and escape the misery of bad judgment and a botched opportunity.

Every time the price moves up and down, new psychological hurdles called support and resistance levels are created. This is nothing more than many people with similar concerns that revolve around common price points. If you can identify these key price points, and take action accordingly, you can benefit from the emotions of others that may have little to do with the company's prospects.

Try to imagine the emotions of buyers and sellers at various points along the way as a chart moves along. What are buyers and sellers feeling today as the indices continue to rally? Are they inclined to sell some positions and take some profits, or are they afraid they are being left behind and are anxious to buy? What are the predominant emotions of the day? Greed? Fear? Relief? If you know where we have been by studying the charts, you will have some good insights into those emotions and how the stock is likely to trade in the future as events unfold.

The reason that charts have meaning is that people remember what they paid for a stock and then go through a series of emotions as they incur profits or losses. Emotions are a rather murky thing, and that means that reading a chart is more of an art than a science. Human behavior has certain tendencies, but it can still be unpredictable at times, which means that charts will never be a perfect way of predicting what will happen in the market.

Before you can fully appreciate the use of charts, it is important to understand that the market does not move randomly. It has a tendency to move in trends. It goes up steadily for a period of time and then goes down steadily for another period of time. Although the general market does not just jump around randomly in a completely unpredictable fashion, it might feel like it. When stocks move in one direction or the other, there is a tendency for that direction to persist for a while.

If you think of the market as being made up of a herd of highly emotional individuals like Mary, this trending action makes sense. People buy or sell because they are influenced by the price action they see. They want to join in the excitement when things are going

up and want to run for safety when they are going down. This causes
the herd mentality, which results in lasting trends.

Whale Watching

Individual investors really have no edge when it comes to analyzing
the fundamental financial characteristics of a stock. There is no way
you can compete against big funds with dozens of full-time analysts
who talk to management and know all the details of a business. You
will never know more about fundamentals than these guys, so why
pretend that you do? What you can do is watch the charts and see if
there are signs that big buyers are interested. If volume picks up and
a stock starts moving, it's probably a sign that someone knows something positive about the fundamental case. When they act, the chart
tells the story.

The use of charts as a predictive tool is an extremely broad and
interesting topic that would take several books to explore in detail.
The key thing to understand about charts is that they tell a story. If we
think about them in terms of emotions and psychology, they can aid
us greatly in figuring where a stock might be headed.

Let's look at a simple but extremely useful aspect of a chart that
can help us decide whether we might like to buy.

Figure 9.9 shows the chart of U.S. Global Investment, Inc., a
company that offers various investment funds. What one thing stands
out the most when you look at this chart?

To me the most interesting thing about this chart is the sudden
surge in volume. Volume went from about 100,000 shares to more
than 10,000,000 shares, and the price went up nearly 50% in the
course of a little more than a week. What happened was that the
company announced a very strong quarterly earnings report—but we
don't even need to know that. What we can see is that a whole lot of
people suddenly wanted this stock and were willing to pay up to get it.

Chart courtesy of TeleChart® by Worden Brothers, Inc. www.worden.com

FIGURE 9.9   The chart of U.S. Global Investment, Inc.

That is the tip-off that the Whales are interested and that the stock is probably worth watching. We might feel a bit uncomfortable jumping in right now, after the stock has already made a move, but let's do what smart Sharks do and start stalking this stock for an entry point.

Over the next few months the stock acts as shown in Figure 9.10.

As you can see, the stock pulled back quite a bit following that big spike on increased volume, but the volume was much lighter, and eventually it started to work back up. If you think about it, this action makes sense from an emotional standpoint. Suddenly, all the folks who had been holding this stock for a long time had a big gain and were probably anxious to cash in. Prior to 2006 the stock had traded for less than $3 since it went public in 1996. When the price hit $16, many probably rushed to lock in gains, and as the stock faded further, other shareholders who still had big gains locked in profits before they faded away.

Chart courtesy of TeleChart® by Worden Brothers, Inc. www.worden.com

FIGURE 9.10   The stock pulled back quite a bit.

Eventually, however, the buyers stepped in because they knew something good was happening. They took advantage of the overanxious folks who were looking to lock in profits and began to accumulate the stock on that pullback. A savvy Shark Investor would be watching for a chance to jump into this stock as the profit-taking dried up and new buyers started to inch in.

As you can see, another big surge in volume occurred in November, and again the stock moved sharply higher. It isn't important to know the details about what caused that interest. All we need to know is that a lot of buyers are eager to jump in, and we might want to continue enjoying the ride.

Figure 9.11 shows what happened next.

Sure enough, the stock continues to trade higher and higher on good volume. In a few months, we could have recognized a substantial profit in this stock simply by paying close attention to the surge in volume and analyzing the emotions that were likely in play.

Chart courtesy of TeleChart® by Worden Brothers, Inc. www.worden.com

FIGURE 9.11   The stock continues to trade higher.

Let's look at another example. Chark Industries (GTLS:Nasdaq) manufactures equipment used in the production and storage of oil and gas. After doing the quick and easy fundamental research discussed in Chapter 11, "Fundamental Analysis: Quick and Easy Is All You Need," we see the stock looks like it has a very attractive valuation. We pull up the chart and see that the stock has been slowly but steadily uptrending for a while. What catches our attention is that every time it pulls back to the 50-day moving average, it finds support and moves higher (see Figure 9.12).

The psychology of what is happening is easy to understand. Buyers want in this stock, but they don't want to chase it higher. Therefore, they stay patient and wait for a pullback. When they don't believe the stock is going to go down much farther, they jump in quickly, and the stock never falls much below the 50-day moving average.

This is an extremely helpful observation because it gives us a good insight into entry points. It also tells us that, if the stock does not bounce back up after hitting the 50-day moving average, something may have changed and we should consider selling and moving on.

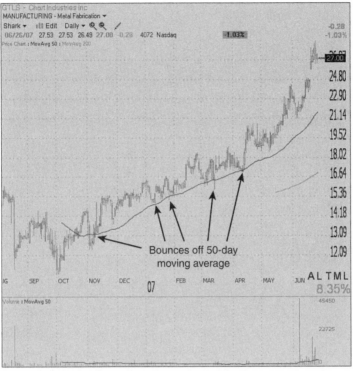

Chart courtesy of TeleChart® by Worden Brothers, Inc. www.worden.com

FIGURE 9.12   The stock consistently bounces off the 50-day moving average.

The Importance of Volume

One of the best and most obvious clues to the emotions and psychology surrounding a stock is volume. When a stock moves on a big surge in volume, that tells us a lot of people are suddenly interested and want to buy shares. Usually some sort of news like a good earnings report or a major contract is the catalyst for the action.

Many investors see a stock move to a new high and think they've missed out. They have been taught to "buy low and sell high" by traditional Wall Street, so they ignore a stock that is up sharply and look for something that is not moving up as strongly.

This is quite often a mistake. A move on a big surge in volume tells us that big money is expecting a continuation of the good news causing this action. Although the academics tell us the market efficiently prices a stock and therefore any good news is fully reflected in the stock immediately, that is not what typically happens. The market tends to be slow in embracing and fully appreciating a stock that is reporting good news. Analysts' estimates tend to inch up only incrementally, and many big funds are interested in buying only after things settle down. The key is that something fundamental is changing, and that typically bodes well for the future, even after a big jump in price.

Figure 9.13 is a chart of Perini Corporation (PCR:NYSE). Perini is a general contractor that builds large projects, such as some of the casinos in Las Vegas. As you can see, the stock jumped up on huge volume in February 2007. The catalyst for the action was a much better than expected earnings report.

Chart courtesy of TeleChart® by Worden Brothers, Inc. www.worden.com

FIGURE 9.13   Perini Corporation jumping in February 2007.

Many investors think it is too late to make money on this stock after the huge move and pass over the situation. Savvy Shark Investors look at it differently. They see the huge volume, review the good news, and then contemplate the psychology. A lot of people obviously want to be in this stock, as evidenced by the giant volume, so they decide to start stalking it and find an entry point. They might take a small initial position and then wait and watch to see how things develop.

Eventually, the stock settles down and pulls back almost exactly to the point where sellers rushed in back in February when the good news first hit (see Figure 9.14). We see that there is a supply of buyers who are supporting the stock and are obviously happy to jump in on this minor weakness. The psychology is that this company is likely to continue to do good things, so we add to our position.

Chart courtesy of TeleChart® by Worden Brothers, Inc. www.worden.com

FIGURE 9.14   The stock pulls back after a big surge in price and volume.

Now it is time to be patient and see if all those anxious buyers who jumped in during February are correct. We are prepared to cut our losses should the stock start to fall back into that gap area on the chart, but otherwise we just bide our time and see how things unfold.

The stock begins to slowly but steadily move up and then explodes higher yet again on another huge surge in volume as the company announces extremely good quarterly earnings once more. The stock rests for a while after that burst of action and then starts to move higher once again, just as it did in March and April (see Figure 9.15).

Volume was the key in tipping us off to the situation. It told us that something good was happening here and that a lot of folks with money wanted to be part of it. All we had to do was follow along for the ride, and we racked up a 50% gain in a matter of a few months.

Chart courtesy of TeleChart® by Worden Brothers, Inc. www.worden.com

FIGURE 9.15   Patience after the volume surge pays off.

Conclusion

These examples should help clarify how useful charts can be as predictive tools. Of course, it is easy for me to pick a good example after the fact. It is a lot harder to do so without the benefit of hindsight. Even the best chart readers are going to get it wrong quite a bit. That is why a portfolio management system that ensures you cut losses quickly and lock in gains before they slip away is so important. We discuss that in detail in the following chapter.

Every stock has a story to tell. We can see the impact of news, the psychology at work, and the emotions at play over time. If we contemplate what investors are thinking and feeling as a stock moves up and down, we gain great insight into how the future might unfold. Even if chart reading weren't so helpful and potentially lucrative, charts ultimately are the study of people and that never is dull or uninteresting.

10

Portfolio Management: The Key to Success

Investment success depends on two basic things: picking good stocks that increase in price, and effectively managing the stocks after you buy them. Effective management means having a plan for either cutting losses or taking gains. Managing your stocks after you buy them is what determines your level of success. Great investing results are a product of shrewd selling rather than smart buying.

All investors will buy their fair share of both good and bad stocks. Even the best investor has plenty of lousy picks along the way, but it is the manner in which you handle those investments after their purchase that ultimately determines your level of success. If you sell your good stocks too early and hold on to your bad stocks too long, it doesn't much matter how good your stock selection might be.

Investors hire stocks to do a job for them, but unfortunately many folks don't bother to manage their stocks after they have been employed. Investors have been influenced by traditional Wall Street to be benign in their attitude toward their stocks. They are undemanding and tend to forgive poor performance. They don't fire a stock from their portfolios until they have to, and usually that happens so late that it ultimately destroys far more capital than necessary.

The Power of Selling

Successful investing is largely the art of selling. Buying a stock is easy. It is determining when to cut our losses or when to take our profits that is hard. Because it is so hard to determine when it is the right time to sell, many folks just don't do it. When in doubt, they do nothing. They just sit and hope that things will eventually work out. Sometimes they do, but many times they don't, and if they don't, it can be quite costly to have left your precious capital tied up in the wrong investment for months or years.

Selling a stock is by far the most valuable tactical tool that the individual investor has at his or her disposal. Selling is cheap and easy and can be undone in the blink of an eye. Too many folks seem to think that if they sell a stock, they are somehow prevented from buying it back again. Not only can you rebuy a stock you sold, but in many cases it may even be a good idea to pay even more than what you just sold it for.

Unfortunately, many on Wall Street make us feel that the word "sell" is the worst four-letter word you can use. As a result, most individual investors tend to think of selling in negative terms. It is considered an admission of failure and something you do only as a last resort when the misery of holding a losing stock becomes too great. Wall Street would have us think that great investors never sell anything, but common sense tells us that is unrealistic and impractical. We hear quite often about the successful investments that Warren Buffett has made, but we seldom hear about stocks he sold, such as Dexter Shoe or Freddie Mac, when it became clear to him that he had made a mistake.

For most investors, the biggest stumbling blocks to selling are mental. A combination of inertia and emotional commitment tends to keep us in a stock we know we should sell. Selling requires that you take action, and investors have a tendency to err on the side of doing nothing when they feel troubled or uncertain. They tell themselves, "I've held on to this stock for this long, and it's been a good performer, so

I might as well continue to hold." Ultimately, that logic leads to giving back big gains and incurring big losses.

Selling Is a Cheap Form of Insurance

The first step in developing a good money management system is to overcome any hesitance about selling. Shark Investors think of selling not as a major commitment but as a form of insurance. If it turns out that your sale was a mistake, buy back the stock even if you pay a little more. Think of that extra cost as an insurance premium.

People in business recognize that they need to regularly spend some money on insurance to protect their businesses against misfortune. The Shark Investor recognizes that he or she needs to spend some money on insurance to protect his or her portfolio. If you think about selling in that way, it is much easier to sell a stock that is acting poorly and then rebuy it when it acts better.

Let's look at an example. Let's say you believe that semiconductors as a group are about to take off, so you purchase the Semiconductor ETF stock (SMH), shown in Figure 10.1. This ETF is just like any other stock, except it combines a dozen or so different semiconductor companies into one stock. As you can see from the chart, the SMH looks like it might finally be moving above the range it has traded in for some time. This would indicate that fresh buying is finally pushing the stock up after a long rest and that it might now begin to gain some upward momentum.

Unfortunately, your timing is off, and soon after you buy shares, the SMH rolls over and starts to trade down. You have two choices at this point: You can hold on and hope that you didn't make a mistake, or you can do the equivalent of buying some insurance and sell some of your holdings.

The Shark Investor has no problem admitting that she might have made a mistake with this buy. She also knows that there is a chance that the stock might continue to fall. Because she is unsure what will happen, she decides to take out some insurance just in case. She sells her shares and takes the $1.50 or so loss.

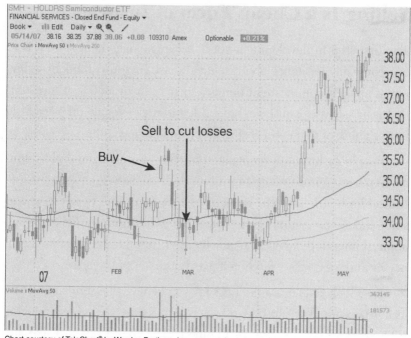

Chart courtesy of TeleChart® by Worden Brothers, Inc. www.worden.com

FIGURE 10.1   The Semiconductor ETF.

Most investors would simply walk away from the situation at this point, but the Shark Investor looks at things differently. That sale was just an insurance policy in case that breakdown in the stock continued. The stock has now found some support. It looks like the original reason we bought was correct, so we rebuy the shares as they start to act they way we thought they would. Although it cost us, and we would have been better off if we had simply held on, we were able to control our risk of loss by using selling as an insurance policy, and now we are making money.

Let's look at another example. A company called iRobot (IRBT), which makes robotic vacuum cleaners, goes public. You've used its product, you think it's pretty clever, and you believe the stock will be a good one to own. You buy shares at about $28 on the day it starts trading. The stock jumps over the next few days, and you are looking pretty smart, but then slowly it starts to pull back. You still have a profit, but it's small. You decide to give the stock some time to prove itself. Over the next month or so the stock begins to move up again, and again you have a good gain. You don't want that profit to slip away this time, so you decide to use a sale as an insurance policy in case the stock trades below the 50-day simple moving average (SMA) that you are tracking on your charts. Your plan is to sell if the stock breaks that point then rebuy later if and when the action is more attractive.

In early February the stock breaks the 50-day simple moving average, and you sell (see Figure 10.2).

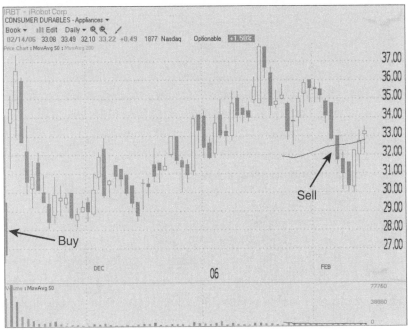

Chart courtesy of TeleChart® by Worden Brothers, Inc. www.worden.com

FIGURE 10.2   Selling iRobot stock.

You continue to watch the stock and are ready to rebuy at a higher price to get back in, because you still think this one may turn out to be a big winner. The stock bounces temporarily but then suddenly collapses and continues to trend down over the next year, as shown in Figure 10.3.

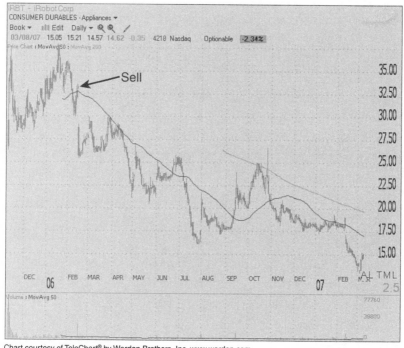

Chart courtesy of TeleChart® by Worden Brothers, Inc. www.worden.com

FIGURE 10.3   iRobot trending down.

Your selling "insurance" in this case protected you from a substantial loss. You would have lost more than half of your capital if you had simply held on to this stock. Instead, you ended up with a better than 10% gain and had the use of those funds for more than a year in other investments that hopefully did much better. When contemplating the value of selling as insurance, it is important not to think of your stocks in isolation but to consider them together. Only when you consider the Semiconductor and iRobot investments together do you really see how cheap selling is as a form of insurance. Yes, the sale cost us something in the SMH situation, but it saved us substantially more in the iRobot situation. But that is how insurance works. It's an irritating expense when we don't need it, but it's a valuable asset to have when we do need it.

The key is to amend your thinking so that you think of selling as nothing more than a form of insurance that you buy when things look dangerous. It might cost you something if your worries prove to be unfounded, but it can save you substantially should disaster hit. Just remember that you can always cancel your insurance by rebuying a stock.

It's Never Too Late to Sell

Investors are often paralyzed into inaction by concluding that it is too late to sell a stock that is already down substantially. This thinking keeps them emotionally and financially tied to underperforming stocks and can cost you substantially while you wait and hope for a recovery.

It is almost never too late to sell a stock in which you have a large loss. You should consider two questions. First, why did you buy this stock? If it was for a fundamental reason, does that reason still exist? Has anything changed? If the stock is down big, something has probably changed. If you bought for technical reasons, you probably were undisciplined and let a loss get out of hand, so you should take the loss and move on.

The second question to consider is whether this stock is the best possible vehicle through which to make up the loss you suffered, or whether you're holding it because you are emotionally invested in it. Just because a stock fell hard and fast doesn't mean it will go up hard and fast when the market is better. So ask yourself if there's a better place for your money than a stock that has caused so much pain. I bet the answer will tend to be yes.

One of the big benefits of selling a stock in which you have a large loss is that it often frees you up mentally and allows you to gain a fresh perspective. When the misery of that big loss is suddenly removed from your brokerage statement, you feel a surge of energy and might be surprised at how readily you can find other opportunities that will help you make up your loss.

Developing a Stock Management System

Now that you appreciate the power of the simple act of using selling as insurance, we can focus on developing a system for managing your stocks that will help you minimize your losses and maximize your gains. Cutting losses quickly and protecting capital is the key to outperforming the market over the long run. The market will always offer us opportunities in which to profit, so we need to make sure we always have capital handy and that it isn't tied up in underperforming stocks. That means we need some sort of framework in which we can systematically make decisions. The best framework for making decisions about your stocks is charts.

Chapter 9, "Charts: Navigating the Market Seas," discussed the basics of charts. It showed how they can be used as predictive tools because they reflect investors' emotions and psychology. Even if you don't want to use charts as predictive tools, they still have tremendous value as a convenient framework in which to manage our investments.

The great benefit of charts is that they help us move in and out of the market systematically as stock prices rise and fall. Where most investors get into trouble is by believing that the stock's price action does not reflect what is really going on there. They think the market is wrong about a stock and ignore weak price action.

One very good example of how focusing on price action rather than fundamentals is the safest approach is to study the trading in the stock of Enron. Enron, which is now defunct, was the largest fraud ever to occur in the United States. The stock was trading as high as 90 in August of 2000 and by January 2002 had fallen to 0.

What is particularly troubling about this situation is that 10 of the 15 analysts following the stock still rated it a "buy" as late as November of 2001, when the stock had fallen to 30.

If you had focused on the fundamental arguments for Enron, you would have continued holding this stock as it lost two-thirds of its value. In retrospect it was obvious that someone knew there was a major problem, and that is why the stock acted so poorly for so long before the real story was finally made public.

If an investor had used rudimentary money management rules in conjunction with the chart, he or she would have been out of Enron well before it blew up.

If you pay attention to the price action on the charts, you have a far better chance of cutting losses at early stages and keeping your capital working hard. You don't have to believe in the value or validity of technical analysis for it to serve a very useful purpose. You just have to appreciate that it provides a set of rules that allow you to manage your portfolio in such a way that you limit losses and protect gains.

Technical analysis is often portrayed as a complex set of tools, composed of intricate calculations. However, it can be easily employed as a simple money management tool that can dramatically increase your returns by helping you avoid substantial losses. Sound impossible? Let's consider another simple example.

As we discussed in the preceding chapter, a simple moving average is a computed average of prices for a given time period displayed through a line attached to a stock's chart. Let's assume that we utilize the 50-day simple moving average as our primary money management tool in deciding when to be invested in the Nasdaq.

Let's assume that each time the Nasdaq closes above the 50-day moving average on a closing basis we will buy, and each time the Nasdaq breaks below the 50-day moving average on a closing basis we will sell.

Figure 10.4 shows what we would have done in 1999 and 2000, when the investing bubble took place.

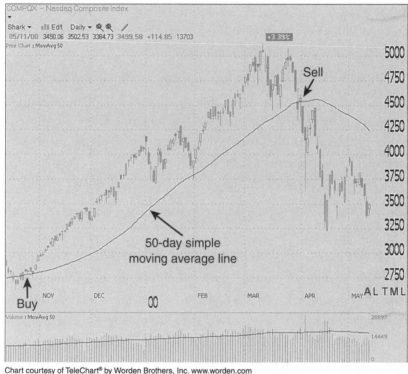

Chart courtesy of TeleChart® by Worden Brothers, Inc. www.worden.com

FIGURE 10.4   The 50-day simple moving average.

As you can see, this strategy would have served you well. You would have caught the majority of the move and then exited within about 10% of the top.

That was a very unusual time in the market, so it's helpful to look at the application of a similar money management system over a ten-year period. Let's again use the system in which we use the 50-day simple moving average to buy and sell, but let's add a condition. We will sell 50% of our position anytime it is more than 10% above the 50-day moving average. The idea is to lock in some gains into strength before they slip away. We will discuss the tactic of making partial sales into strength later in this chapter in the "Partial Buys and Partial Sells" section.

Figure 10.5 compares the buy-and-hold (B&H) approach versus the money management (MM) approach by year since 1996.

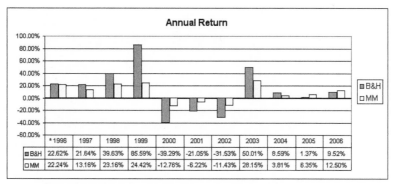

Chart courtesy of TeleChart® by Worden Brothers, Inc. www.worden.com

FIGURE 10.5   Money management versus buy and hold: annual returns.

As you can see, the buy-and-hold system did extremely well in 1999, when the market was going straight up. But the money management approach did far better in 2000 through 2003, when the market was struggling. Overall you might not think that the money management system provided that much of an advantage. It certainly helped more when things were rough, but it didn't help very much when times were good.

What you have to realize is how valuable it is to not lose money when the market is acting poorly. If you lose money, you are handicapped, because you have to make up those losses before you can start to generate profits again. For example, if you start with $10,000 and lose $2,000, you need a gain of 25% before you are back to even. If you lose $5,000, you need a gain of 100% before you return to even. Then you can start making money again. Making up those losses is tremendously costly and unproductive. Rather than adding to your top line, you are simply repeating what you have already done.

With that in mind, let's consider the cumulative returns produced by our simple money management system versus the buy-and-hold approach (see Figure 10.6).

As you can see, the money management system produced returns of 264.72% over the ten-year period versus just 129.41% for the buy-and-hold approach. The primary reason for the big difference is that the money management system lost far less money during the poor market of 2000 to 2003. Because it wasn't necessary to recoup as many losses, it was far easier to build capital at a compounded rate when the market started to act better in 2004.

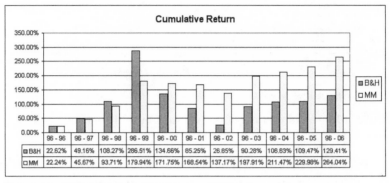

Chart courtesy of TeleChart® by Worden Brothers, Inc. www.worden.com

FIGURE 10.6   Money management versus buy and hold: cumulative returns.

There are a number of other considerations here as well. The money management system is far less risky than the buy-and-hold system, because there are times when you are not in the market at all. If you aren't in the market, you have no chance of suffering losses due to some extraneous event like 9/11 or a market crash. In addition, during the times you have idle cash, you can earn interest on that money by putting it in a money market account or certificate of deposit.

The money management system may result in higher transaction costs, because you are making more trades. But with commission costs so low, that is generally not an issue unless you are using a very small amount of capital. If you aren't trading in a tax-advantaged account like an IRA, you may also have to consider the impact of paying taxes earlier than you might otherwise. An accurate analysis of how taxes might impact the results would depend on a wide variety of factors. But even in the worst circumstances it is extremely unlikely that the after-tax results would be better with the buy-and-hold approach.

Now that you understand the power of a simple money management system, you need to work on developing some approaches to determining when you will exit a stock you have bought. You have three basic choices: using a flat percentage stop loss; using moving averages (as just demonstrated with the money management system); or using support levels, trend lines, or other aspects of a chart.

A *flat percentage stop loss* approach is probably the easiest money management system to use. It is nothing more than automatically selling a stock every time you reach a certain threshold of loss. Typically when using this approach, an investor sells his stock when he has an 8 to 10% loss. For example, if you buy a stock at $30, you would sell if it pulled back to between $27 and $27.60.

Much study has been done on the ultimate stop-loss percentage to use, but there is no clear answer. The problem is that if you set your stops too tight or too close, you run the risk that you will sell a good stock simply due to ordinary volatility. If you set your stops too far away or too loose, you will suffer greater losses before you eventually sell.

What works best varies widely. If you invest in conservative, slower-moving blue-chip stocks, the best stop-loss percentage is quite different than if you invest in volatile, fast-moving stocks. At certain times, the volatility in the market may make tight stops work better than loose stops, or vice versa.

Trying to determine the best percentage to use for a stop is so difficult that it is probably better to start with an arbitrary level such as 8% and then contemplate a variation as soon as you see how that works with your particular style of investing.

A somewhat more complex selling methodology is to use the *moving average* approach discussed in the preceding money management example. Several considerations here are similar to those we face when using a stop-loss percentage. If we use a very short moving average, we are much more likely to have it triggered due to ordinary volatility, which takes us out of a stock at a bad time. Figure 10.7 shows an example using Cisco.

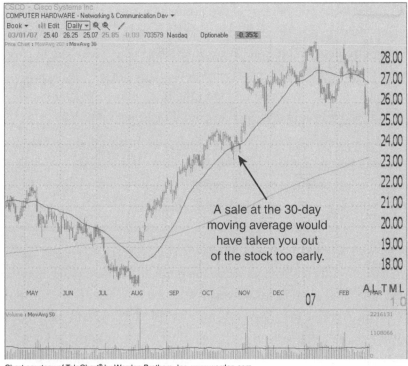

Chart courtesy of TeleChart® by Worden Brothers, Inc. www.worden.com

FIGURE 10.7   The moving average approach.

With the 50-day moving average as our sell trigger, we would maximize our gains in CSCO (Cisco Systems), as shown in Figure 10.8.

With the 30-day moving average, we would have sold prematurely. However, if the stock had continued down at that point, it would have been better to use the shorter moving average.

The third approach to selling is to use *trend lines, support levels,* and other aspects of the chart that might indicate that the character of the price action is changing. Stocks have a tendency to trend. As soon as a stock starts moving in a certain direction, that move often persists over a period of time. There are a number of reasons for this, but it's primarily due to our human inclination to worry that we are missing out as a stock begins to move. The more people we see enjoying the party, the more inclined we are to jump in as well, and that can feed on itself for a long time. Eventually the move comes to an end, but riding the trend can be tremendously profitable as long as you hold on to your gains by jumping out as soon as things begin to break down.

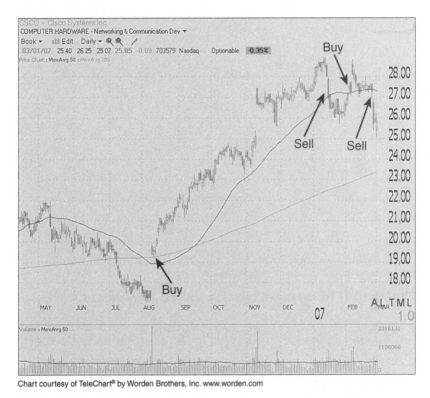

Chart courtesy of TeleChart® by Worden Brothers, Inc. www.worden.com

FIGURE 10.8   Maximizing gains in Cisco using the 50-day moving average.

Figure 10.9 shows how riding recent trends in the Dow Jones Industrial Average has worked.

As you can see, by simply watching the trend lines and selling when they were breached, you could have racked up some big gains. You would have had to sell and rebuy a couple times, but as we discussed earlier, that would have been cheap insurance. If you can exit quickly and preserve your gains, you can reenter much more easily and continue to grow your account.

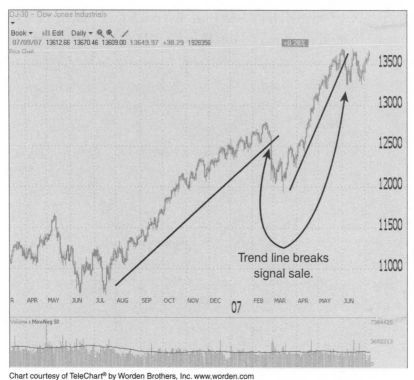

Chart courtesy of TeleChart® by Worden Brothers, Inc. www.worden.com

FIGURE 10.9   Riding recent trends in the Dow Jones Industrial Average.

Another approach to using charts as a management tool is to consider what are called support and resistance levels. These are places on the charts where the stock has traded for a long time. That is important, because it tells us that many people have established a position at a certain price and therefore they are likely to have somewhat similar reactions as the stock moves away from that point.

Figure 10.10 shows the chart of Dell Computers.

As you can see, during almost all of 2004, Dell traded in a fairly narrow range. Most of the investors in the stock would have bought at about a price of $33 to $35. Subsequently, the stock moved out of that trading range and hit new highs in 2005. Folks who bought in 2004 probably felt pretty good that they saw some gains, but a number of others who bought then probably sold.

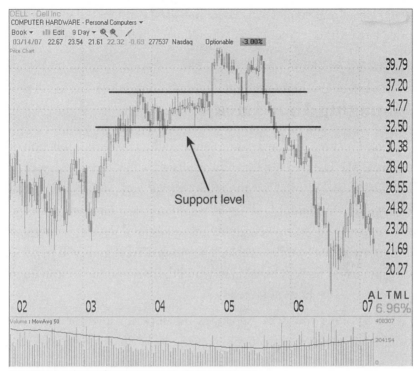

Chart courtesy of TeleChart® by Worden Brothers, Inc. www.worden.com

FIGURE 10.10   The Dell Computers chart.

In 2006 the stock started to fall sharply, and the holders from 2004 began to see their unrealized gains slip away. That support level is important psychologically, because it indicates the point where all buyers since 2003 will suffer a loss. When people have a loss in a stock, they are much more inclined to sell than if they have a gain, so you need to take note of that point. If you are holding this stock, you want to consider exiting as soon as it looks like that psychological shift is likely to occur.

As you can see, the selling eventually overwhelmed the stock after it broke through that support level, and it traded substantially lower.

Most stock charts contain a psychological or emotional story like this that can be a handy guide to knowing when things are changing and that it may be time to sell. Just consider the emotional reactions you might have if you bought at a certain time, and consider the subsequent price moves. It is a great help in deciding when to make a sale.

Managing Your Luck

To a great degree, our success or failure in the market is a function of our luck. We like to think that our results are a direct consequence of our insight and efforts, but the reality is that luck plays a big part in how we do. No matter how smart we are, or how hard we work, we will regularly be hit by news, circumstances, and developments that are unforeseen and unknowable. The stock market gods will periodically use us for their entertainment, and there is nothing we can do to prevent it, so we have to be ready.

In the long run, what separates the superior investor from the pack is the ability to effectively manage luck. Shark investors know that sometimes they will have streaks of bad luck, and other times everything they touch is golden.

The key is to survive your runs of bad luck with the minimum amount of damage and to capitalize when your luck is good. We have already discussed how an aggressive approach toward selling and the use of charts as a selling framework can help you escape when things turn sour, but that isn't enough.

In designing a money management system, your first consideration should be how well it protects your capital should you have a run of bad luck. If the positions you are holding are too big, then you run the risk that one or two bad stocks can cause major damage. If your stops are too loose, that allows losses to grow too big and that can impair your capital and jeopardize your ability to produce gains in the future. As we discussed earlier, having to recover from substantial losses wastes time and requires much work just to get back to even. If we own five stocks and set our stop-loss percentage at 20%, chances are we will take a substantial hit in sudden market weakness.

On the other hand, if we are too cautious and our position sizes are too small and/or our stops too tight, we will fail to capitalize when good luck is running. If we buy and hold just one really great stock, we have a chance of producing a fantastic return, but if we are wrong, the damage can be devastating.

Most market participants learn quickly that they should follow the adage about not putting all their eggs in one basket. Diversification is a key attribute of any money management system. If you invest in a number of different stocks, that greatly cuts the risk that any one investment will impair your capital.

The number one rule of money management is to stay diversified. I typically don't have any one position that is greater than 5 to 10% of my capital. I know there will be unexpected news, analyst downgrades, or earnings preannouncements, or that I might have just made a mistake. Everyone gets caught in an ugly situation from time to time. This is unavoidable. The key is not to let any one stock be capable of doing you any real damage. It will still sting when you are caught by surprise, but you won't substantially impair your capital, and if you are diversified, you can shake it off and move forward.

Sometimes it can be tempting to make a big bet on one stock that you feel strongly about: "This one will make up for the last five stupid buys I made." Resist that temptation. The goal is to stay in the game for the very long run, not to try to hit home runs. When you swing for the fences, you run the risk of striking out. In investing, when you strike out and lose your capital, the game is over.

So how many stock positions should you hold? As I mentioned, I almost never put more than 5% of my capital in one stock. Therefore, if I am heavily invested, I will be holding more than 20 stocks. If you are working with smaller amounts of cash, you want to set a certain minimum size so that transaction costs don't eat up your gains. If you are buying just $100 worth of stock, you might need a 10% move just to break even after commissions and other costs. It is better to set your minimum investment size at $1,000 so that the transaction costs are irrelevant. If you are operating with $10,000 to $20,000, you might hold five to ten stocks, with no one being less than $1,000 and no one being greater than $3,000 to $4,000.

The amount of capital you use has a major impact on how diversified your holdings are. The more money you are working with, the more stocks you are likely to hold. However, a trade-off occurs at some point. If you hold too many stocks, eventually you will just mimic an index, and it will be difficult to produce better-than-average returns. In addition, it can be quite difficult to effectively manage hundreds of positions. There is great danger of diminished returns when you are overdiversified.

Aside from capital, the other things you need to consider when determining the number of stocks to own are the types of stocks you are holding, your time frames, and your investing style.

If you tend to favor highly volatile small caps, you will likely want to be more diversified than someone who is holding big, slow-moving blue chips. The more risk your average stock carries, the more you want to make sure you have other stocks to protect you in case something goes wrong.

Another important consideration in determining your level of diversification is your style of investing. Highly aggressive investors who watch the stock market closely may feel much more comfortable with concentrated exposure in a smaller group of stocks than a longer-term investor who holds more conservative stocks. However, be careful in concluding that your big blue-chip stocks will protect you. As we've discussed, they can languish for many years and cause massive under-performance if they are too big a percentage of your portfolio.

Diversifying by Time Frame

One often-overlooked approach to being diversified is to invest in the same stock in a variety of time frames. This is generally accomplished by trading around a "core" long-term position. A core position is simply a stock that you feel has good prospects and that you are willing to hold for the longer term to give it a chance to work. After you establish a position in a stock and follow it over time, you become familiar with the stock's "personality." This makes it possible to identify shorter-term opportunities for profit. Although there is still a higher level of risk when you hold a large position in a single stock, it is decreased if you plan on being in it for only a limited time.

This approach can help you add to your overall returns as you become adept at moving in and out of the stock in question. Some active traders make a living doing just this with a small group of select stocks that they know very well.

Time-frame diversification is also useful when you feel uncertain about the market environment. Perhaps you have doubts about the market's health in the intermediate term, but in the short term it is acting well. Adopting a temporary shorter-term approach allows you to keep your risk in tune with your overall investment approach.

Partial Buys and Partial Sells

How would your investing change if you knew without a doubt that you couldn't time the market precisely? You can't time the market precisely, but most investors like to think they can. Rather than waste time on an impossible task, we simply need to find a way to take into account that our timing will always be off to some degree when we buy or sell a stock. The best way to handle this uncertainty is to hedge by averaging into and out of positions over time and by allowing yourself some reasonable amount of room for error. You'd be a little early and a little late and would be disinclined to use an all-or-nothing approach to your investments. You won't get it exactly right, but you try to get reasonably close by taking a more incremental approach.

Unfortunately, most investors worry too much about exact timing and often miss out. Either they are too aggressive too early and then are forced to sell when the stock doesn't cooperate as they hoped, or they are too aggressive too late and end up missing the meat of a move. The better approach is often to be a little early and a little late.

I seldom make one buy and one sale of a stock. My methodology is to average in and average out of a stock and to use varying time frames. I constantly evaluate my positions as conditions evolve. The partial-buy-and-sell strategy helps smooth out my mistakes on entry and exit points. The only way you usually catch the optimal entry point is purely by luck. If I average into a position over time, the fact that my timing is off to some degree is diminished. I have no qualms about paying more or less than my original price as long as the reason for buying the stock remains in place.

The partial-buy-and-sell strategy is also a good way to diversify over time frames. I can sell a portion for a quick gain if it goes my way, or cut my losses quickly if I'm wrong. At the same time, I can use looser stops and be patient with a portion for a longer term to see if it plays out the way I anticipated.

Figure 10.11 shows a stock to which I applied the partial-buy-and-sell approach.

As you can see, my initial buys proved to be poorly timed. I had bought on a sharp spike higher following a good earnings report. The stock reversed abruptly and proceeded to trade down for a couple weeks subsequently. If I had bought too much too early, I probably would have sold and taken a loss on some of the shares. Instead, I planned to add shares, so the pullback was actually welcomed rather than a source of frustration.

Eventually the stock started to turn up, and I was able to slowly sell down the portion of the shares I was holding with a shorter time frame. I continued to hold my core position and ended up augmenting my profit greatly with the incremental buys and sells.

It is important to understand the difference between averaging in to establish a new position and averaging down into a losing position. I seldom average down; I almost always average in. This might seem like a distinction without a real difference, but to me the difference is like night and day.

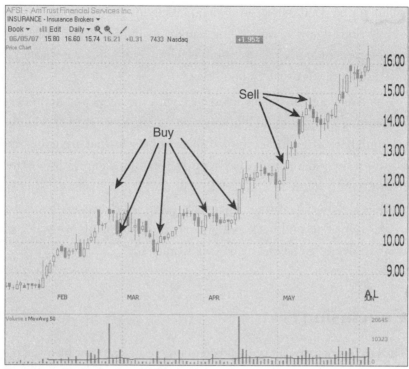

Chart courtesy of TeleChart® by Worden Brothers, Inc. www.worden.com

FIGURE 10.11   The partial-buy-and-sell approach.

When you average into a stock, you have a plan of attack in mind. You will buy a certain amount of this stock, and you will do so by making this many buys. Averaging down is an emotional reaction after the fact to a stock that is not doing what you hoped. You want to believe that you made a good decision, so you add to the position, even though you never intended to. Averaging down is emotional and reactive, whereas averaging in is planned in advance and strategic.

The biggest losses that most investors sustain come from averaging down in an attempt to catch a bottom in a stock. The problem comes when they keep adding more and more because they are so confident that things will reverse at any time. When the stock continues to sink, it becomes impossible for those investors to extricate themselves from the deep, dark hole. In many cases these stocks that seem to be falling for no good reason are indeed falling for good reasons that we simply don't know about. Being caught in one of these situations can be tremendously painful. That is why averaging down without a preexisting play is usually a poor idea.

One difficulty many investors face with the averaging in process is that they have a mental block against paying more than their original purchase price for additional shares of stocks that are going up. We all want a bargain, so we keep waiting and hoping for better prices. Quite often it is better to pay up for more shares when a stock is stubbornly strong. There are often good reasons behind a stock's refusal to pull back and give us the entry points we want, so don't be averse to paying up as you average in.

Conclusion

The key to stock market success is properly managing your investments after you buy them. The way to do that is fairly simple:

- Don't be afraid to sell. Think of selling as a form of insurance.
- Have a methodology that clearly establishes exit points.
- Diversify by stock as well as time frame.
- Use a partial-buy and partial-sell approach.

In baseball, there is much debate over whether it is better to hit for an average or for power. Players who swing for the fences end up striking out a lot and tend to have lower batting averages, but they make up for it by putting runs on the scoreboard when they do connect. The stock market is quite different. Swinging for the fences when you are investing can carry a much higher price than a simple strikeout. If you bet too big and too aggressively, you risk not only striking out but losing the game.

In investing the game is over if you lose or impair your capital to a great degree. Having sufficient capital is the key to more appearances at the plate. If you have enough times at bat, you will eventually connect. Without capital, you are on the bench and have no chance of making money. Guard that capital zealously by using the money management principles we have discussed. If you have capital to work with, there will always be opportunities to make money in the stock market.

11

Fundamental Analysis: Quick and Easy Is All You Need

I have often made substantial money investing in a stock even though I knew nothing about it other than its name and trading symbol. I simply let the chart be my guide and acted as it instructed. My thinking was that the chart indicates that someone knows something about this stock that is quite positive, so why don't I just go along for the ride?

Traditional Wall Street generally is appalled by such an approach. They consider it dangerous, lazy, and lacking in intellectual rigor. The conventional belief is that you should buy stocks only after doing complete and through fundamental analysis and not bother at all with those silly squiggly lines on the chart.

Fundamental analysis involves researching a business's earnings, balance sheet, management, and various other aspects. It is an attempt to determine a company's value by analyzing the business and then comparing it to the stock price to see whether it is a good value. The theory is that if a stock is a good value, eventually the market will recognize that fact and drive up the price to where it should be. It might take months or years, but if you are right, eventually it should pay off.

As we have discussed, trying to beat the Whales of Wall Street by doing fundamental analysis of this type is a nearly impossible task for the average individual investor. The big mutual funds, institutions, and brokers simply have the resources and abilities to do a much better job of it than we ever can. They have large staffs with big budgets and easy access to senior management that allow them to obtain detailed information and insights that the average investor could never obtain.

Because the playing field is not level when it comes to doing effective fundamental analysis, savvy Shark Investors focus primarily on price action and always defer to what the charts tell them. Ultimately the actions that Whales take because of the results of their fundamental research are reflected in the charts. If they think a stock is a good one, they buy. Because they are so big, that buying affects the price. This shows up in the price action and volume on the charts and allows Shark Investors to jump in and follow along if we like.

Even though most fundamental analysis doesn't give the individual investor any great edge, it still can be a helpful adjunct to using charts. It can provide some added confidence and insight as you consider how to handle a particular stock.

For example, the market quite often favors a particular sector, such as China stocks, alternative energy, semiconductors, oil, or retailers. Sectors tend to go through rotations, with various ones leading and lagging at certain times, so knowing something about your stock's business and sector is helpful. In addition, when one stock in an industry has good news, you can sometimes profit by buying other stocks in the same industry as prices rise in sympathy. If you already are familiar with an industry's stocks, it's easier to move quickly when a sector is favored by the market.

Another advantage of fundamental research is that the Whales don't actively research and study many of the smaller stocks. Therefore, you can uncover some facts and insights that are not widely known and efficiently priced into a stock. A stock like Starbucks, which has about 20 analysts following it, or Dell Computers, which has 26 analysts, will not offer an opportunity for an individual looking to uncover something that was overlooked. However, many smaller stocks are not covered by analysts or have very limited coverage. There still is plenty of big smart money out there that is likely to do better research than we can, but it is not quite as competitive in some cases. It is possible to uncover some interesting fundamental facts that are not widely known.

Fundamental Research to Determine a Stock's Value Is Just a Guess

One of the deceptive things about fundamental research is that it isn't the precise science that it might seem to be. Although analyzing balance sheets and developing complex spread sheets of projected earning trends produces lots of hard numbers, a tremendous amount of guess work is still involved. No one ever knows for sure what will happen in the future, and quite often the most rigorous examination of a company results in wildly inaccurate predictions about the future of a stock. Even a company's top management can have difficulty predicting what the future holds for their business. So how can a third party who doesn't have the intimate familiarity with the company do a better a job?

Even if you can develop good insights and financial models into future earning trends, you still don't know what valuation the market will assign to a stock. In theory, the value of a stock is the discounted present value of its future earnings stream. In other words, a stock is worth what it will earn in the future but reduced by an amount equal to what you would earn on your money if it was invested in a bond or a bank account.

That means to determine a fair price for a stock you need to know not only what future earnings will be but also what an appropriate discount rate or interest rate should be. Stock prices are largely a function of interest rates. When interest rates are high, the money that will be earned several years from now is worth less in today's dollars. This means a stock will be worth less. When interest rates are low, stocks are generally worth more because the money they earn several years from now is worth more.

When you consider that you need to predict both what a stock is going to earn in the future and also what interest rates are going to do, it becomes pretty clear that fundamental analysis is not the hard science Wall Street would have you believe.

Analyzing Earnings to Gain Confidence in Your Stock Picks

Even if you are inclined to do fundamental research, spending weeks and months investigating a stock is not feasible or particularly productive for the average investor. It might yield some interesting insights, but it is tremendously difficult, time-consuming, and hard work.

Shark Investors realizes that some insight into fundamentals can be helpful, but they want to limit their work to focusing on just a few of the most important things that can be determined quickly and easily. You don't want to get caught up in minutiae that don't matter much in the bigger scheme of things. You want to understand the big picture and the potential drivers of higher prices. Digging into balance sheets, running projections, and reading hundreds of pages of SEC filings can generate interesting details, but ultimately there are secondary considerations. The number one thing that drives a stock price is earnings—specifically, how fast earnings are likely to grow in the future compared to present expectations. The faster earnings are growing and the lower the expectations, the higher a stock will likely move. So you want to find a stock that is growing earnings very quickly but whose price doesn't fully reflect its likely future growth. This can be determined in a fairly quick and easy way. The first step is to determine the current valuation of a stock. This is done by calculating its P/E ratio. The P stands for price, and the E stands for earnings. Thus, a P/E of 10 means that a stock's price is 10 times its earnings. A stock with a P/E of 20 means that the stock is valued at 20 times earnings over the past year. The P/E ratio for any stock can be found on financial sites like Yahoo! Finance and Google Finance.

The general idea behind the P/E ratio is that a stock is an attractive value if it trades at a low ratio. If a company earns one dollar in a year and trades at a price of 12, its P/E ratio would be 12. At first glance, this would be considered "cheaper" than another stock that earns a dollar and sells for a price of 20. However, assuming that the stock with a P/E ratio of 12 is a better bargain is not necessarily correct.

Unfortunately, many people make the mistake of thinking that a high P/E is bad and a low P/E is good. That is not necessarily the case. In fact, the opposite quite often occurs. P/E ratios are not inherently bad or good. What matters is how they compare to projected future earnings growth rates. If a stock has a high P/E ratio but even higher future growth, that may represent a better value than a stock with a low P/E and no earnings growth.

The relationship between P/E and growth is key. Shark Investors can quickly calculate that number to give themselves a feel for how cheap or expensive a stock might be. The lower the P/E compared to the future growth, the better. Ideally I like to see projected growth at twice the trailing P/E; however, it is difficult to find stocks that meet that test, and I am often satisfied with something much less.

Let's look at a couple of examples. Let's assume that a company earned 55 cents over the last 12 months, and the stock's price is $15.39. If we divide the price by the earnings, we get a P/E ratio of about 28. That may sound a little high for an average stock but let's look at the growth rate.

We pull up Yahoo! Finance and see that the company expects to earn 93 cents in the coming year and $1.48 in the year after that. An increase in earnings from 55 cents to 93 cents is 69% growth. A further jump to $1.48 the next year would be an additional 48% increase in earnings. So we do a little math and determine that over the next two years earnings are expected to grow at a compounded rate of 64%. 64% growth compared to a P/E ratio of 28 is better than 2 to 1, so this stock appears to be quite cheap.

Another way to look at this situation is to assume that the P/E ratio remains the same over the next two years. If it stays at 28 and the company earns the $1.48 that is expected two years from now, the price of the stock would be 28 × $1.48, or $41.44, which would be a very nice gain form the present price of $15.39.

It is very unlikely that the P/E ratio would remain that high unless the company's earnings growth is expected to increase even more in the years ahead. However, this illustrates the potential price increase should the market start to recognize that this stock is a "bargain."

Of course, it is possible that the earnings estimates we have used in our calculations may be incorrect. That is why ultimately we have to defer to the price action we see on the chart. If this stock, with this seemingly cheap valuation, starts to act weak, then we need to be careful. One of the easiest ways to suffer a big loss is to ignore poor price action because of earnings estimates that then turn out to be completely wrong.

On the other hand, if the stock is acting well, quick and easy fundamental research can give us confidence to add more shares and to hold on longer as we watch the stock appreciate. Knowing that a stock that has a good chart and is acting well is also "cheap" on a fundamental basis allows us to be more aggressive and to potentially profit to a greater degree.

Now let's look at a very different situation. Coca-Cola is a huge, well-established company with a steady and predictable flow of earnings. Coca-Cola is trading at a price of $52 and has earned $2.37 over the last year. That gives us a P/E ratio of 22. Sixteen analysts follow the stock, and on average they estimate that Coca-Cola will grow earnings by about 10% a year for the next two years.

So the growth of Coca-Cola is roughly one-half of its P/E ratio. That is a substantial difference from the preceding example, where the growth rate is roughly 4 times the P/E ratio. There are a number of reasons for this discrepancy, such as the steadiness and consistency of Coca-Cola's earnings compared to the more cyclical and volatile previous example. But obviously the potential for price appreciation is far greater for the stock with the high growth compared to its P/E versus the much more conservative and more fully valued Coca-Cola.

Conclusion

We could continue to dig and do further research into the details of a company's business, but this quick-and-dirty calculation of growth to P/E tells us much of what we need to know. If the growth is high compared to the P/E, we might be more aggressive in pursuing the stock. If the ratio of growth to P/E is low, we might be less forgiving and more inclined to sell quickly should the stock start not acting well. Fundamental research can give us greater confidence as we ponder how to handle our investment in a particular stock.

For just about every stock I buy, I try to gain a quick understanding of the overall business, and then I do the P/E ratio-to-growth-rate comparison. I might still invest in a stock just because I like the chart, but knowing these two additional factors gives me a bit more comfort and confidence when I want to act.

The key thing that Shark Investors stay focused on is that even if we think a stock's fundamental situation is good, we still need the market to verify our insight. Legions of stocks are great values but languish for months or years. We can't rely on calculations of growth rates and P/Es alone. We also need some sign in the chart that the market is taking note.

So do some quick and easy fundamental research, because it might give you a further edge. But don't forget that someone with a lot more money always knows much more about a stock than you do. Watch what that person does by watching the charts, and don't think you will outsmart him or her through fundamental research.

12

Developing Your Inner Shark

Shark Investing is not a rigid, structured approach to the stock market with an unvarying set of rules. It is a mind-set that frees investors from the constraints of traditional Wall Street thinking and focuses on using the flexibility and the many advantages that the average individual investor possesses. There are many ways to be a successful stock market Shark; what works best is highly subjective. What works best for me might not work best for you, and vice versa.

As discussed in Chapter 6, "The Myths of Wall Street," no approach to the market is inherently superior. What works best depends more on the makeup of the individual than on what is actually being done. A good chart reader might outperform a poor fundamental investor, and a good fundamental investor might outperform a good chart reader.

Most market participants have a tendency to be defensive when it comes to their particular approach to the market. If they didn't believe their approach was the best way to make money, they wouldn't be using it. However, they make the mistake of projecting their own situation and feelings on to others and don't appreciate how someone else might have trouble duplicating their approach.

Many Wall Street professionals are downright snide when it comes to people who approach the market differently than they do. You will quite often hear jokes and insults about those goofy investors who use charts or have a short-term approach. Wall Street is not open-minded when it comes to nontraditional investment approaches.

There is no doubt in my mind that I produce far better results with my nontraditional, chart reading/small cap/momentum style than I would if I tried a longer-term fundamental approach. But I'm very aware that it might not be as easy for folks who don't think like I do, who don't have my emotional makeup, and who don't actively follow the market like I do.

Developing your particular Shark Style involves three key considerations. The amount of time you want to dedicate to investing will determine how much research you might do and how closely you monitor your holdings, which will determine the length of your holdings periods. Your emotional and psychological makeup will help determine if you have the temperament to play fast-moving, volatile stocks or are better suited to looking for undiscovered gems that will slowly gain attention. Your skill set will determine if you will dig into financial statements, study the science behind biotechnology stocks, or focus on using charts to measure emotions.

The most important thing is to know yourself and to keep trying various things until you arrive at an approach that works. Unfortunately, the market often makes that quite difficult, because it is always changing, so the things that work best during one period may change. However, that doesn't mean that you reinvent yourself every time you struggle a bit. After you develop a style, it is important to stick with it and not give up just because you don't make immediate progress.

We all have different levels of risk tolerance, patience, activity, and emotional ups and downs. What is comfortable for one investor will drive another to distraction. If you can appreciate that fact, arriving at a style that works for you is easier.

One mistake that many new investors make is trying to exactly duplicate what someone else is doing. If you want to do that, you should just hire that person to manage your money, and find something else to do with your time. It has always been my contention that investors need to find a style that works best for them. No style is inherently superior. Be it fundamental, technical, momentum, value, or whatever, success depends on your ability to properly execute. Strive to develop your own personal style of investing that is comfortable for you.

In finding your personal investing style, your first step is to understand what your ultimate goals are. If you are competing against institutional investors and funds, you probably will focus on beating the indices. If you are trading to pay your monthly bills, you are likely to focus on quick gains and capital preservation. Once you are clear on what you want to obtain from the market, you can work on developing your style.

Before we talk about some specific Shark Investing styles, let's do a little self-analysis. You must understand yourself before you know what will work best for you.

The first question that comes to mind as we consider how we will attack the market is whether good investors are made or born. Do successful investors possess some innate ability, or can anyone who is reasonably intelligent and has a good work ethic learn how to be an exceptional investor? Generally, anyone can learn how to invest fairly well, but what really determines someone's success is what is known as "emotional intelligence." That term was popularized by Daniel Goleman in a number of books and articles and is an attempt to look beyond cognitive capacity measured by IQ and to focus on the various abilities and traits that each of us possesses.

The best investors have high emotional intelligence. They are acutely aware of their own feelings of fear and greed and can deal with them objectively. They know their strengths and weaknesses and are very aware of them. In addition, they can see those things in other people and have the ability to view emotions dispassionately.

The capacity to understand and deal with your emotional strengths, weaknesses, and inclinations is critical to a high level of success as an investor. Some folks simply cannot control their propensity to be overly conservative or aggressive or whatever. They may know all the investing rules and tricks, but their inability to recognize and deal with their emotions keeps them from succeeding.

Market participants tend to underestimate the importance of their emotions when making market decisions. If you have a totally mechanical or mathematical approach to the market, you don't have to worry too much about pesky emotions. However, many investors, including myself, employ a less objective approach to the market. Good investors tend to be amateur psychologists. Not only can they understand the emotions that are driving the market, they also can objectively consider their own emotions and feelings when the impulse to act occurs.

When you are trying to make decisions about the market based on your view of the prevailing mood, sentiment, and/or psychology, you have to be particularly aware of how your feelings affect your thought process. This is true whether you are making money, struggling with big losses, or riding a long winning or losing streak. Emotions color your attitude toward the market and often push you to act when feelings of fear or greed overcome logic. Self-awareness is a valuable trait to cultivate in many areas of life. Investing is no different.

The role of emotions becomes even more important when the market has been trending down. When investors have large unrealized losses in a poor market environment, this can greatly impair their objectivity. They struggle to reassure themselves about why they bought a particular stock. They can bring themselves to admit defeat and sell only when the losses are so big they can't bear to take the pain any longer. Investors frequently wrestle with whether they should dump a weak position or wait it out and hope for a rebound.

As you consider that decision, it is a good time to do an emotional inventory of your thought process. Are you holding on to a weak position because it's difficult for you to admit being wrong? Are you selling a good position because you are just generally feeling fearful or worried without any real reason? Are you holding onto something because you've held it for a long time and are emotionally attached to it? Are you dumping things in a methodical and disciplined manner, or are you burying your head in the sand, holding onto stock you shouldn't and ignoring reality? It's a cliché to say you need to be in touch with your feelings, but this is true when it comes to investing. We all have impulses to do things, and many times they are not in our best interest. If you can take the time to objectively consider what you are feeling, you will be a better investor.

When the market is tough, we often hear how we should "be tough," "suck it up," "take the pain," and a variety of other macho blandishments. Being tough and brave is a good thing in many situations, but the stock market isn't one of them. In fact, I'll go so far as to claim that a smart wimp who runs and hides when the going gets tough generally produces better results than brave souls who are proud of their ability to suffer great monetary pains while they wait for their convictions to be rewarded.

The problem with the "macho" approach to the markets is that the consequences of being wrong are so onerous. The stronger your convictions and beliefs, the more invested and braver you are, and the greater the chance for a backbreaking loss. The wimpy investor knows that the key to success is staying in the game for the very long term. Bravery can pay off nicely at times, but it can also cause you some grave injuries.

Don't be too fast to discount your feelings and emotions. Good investing requires a healthy emotional state. When we are tired, sick, depressed, or just plain weary from an uncooperative market, we are prone to making bad decisions and doing things we normally wouldn't. Treat yourself gently when the going is tough and you are tired. Take time to recharge and build your emotional capital. It will pay off in the long run. Stay cognizant of your emotions. If you are feeling troubled and uncertain or confident and cocky, be quick to identify this, and keep it in mind as you decide how to trade.

Don't project your emotional state onto the market. Many of our biases and inclinations are subtle and difficult to deal with. A habit that I still have to deal with regularly is an inclination to take profits too quickly. I had to ask myself what in my thinking led me to act that way. The answer was that I simply didn't have confidence that a move would continue. I was imposing my judgment on the market about what I thought was a "reasonable" advance. My feelings about what constituted a sufficient move in a stock were at odds with the market. I often found it difficult to adjust my concept of a move's "reasonableness," so I developed a strategy in which I would make partial sales of a stock and hold on to a portion, even though I felt the stock was too extended. Basically, this was a form of behavior modification. As I experienced success in holding on longer than I felt comfortable, I became capable of greater patience.

The following comment about hedge fund manager Steven A. Cohen in the *New York Times* is of particular interest to investors. He is regarded by many as one of the best traders operating today: "Part of what makes Mr. Cohen such an accomplished trader is his equanimity. He rarely shouts or yells, just processes information and marshals his order flow to the 70 portfolio managers who work with him. People who have seen him trade say it is impossible to tell whether he is having the best or the worst day of his life at any given moment in the course of a day."[1]

The lesson is that successful investors take the ups and downs of investing in stride. They don't let the bad days make them depressed, and they don't get euphoric when they have a good day. They know that some of each will occur in the normal course of business, and they accept that fact and keep plugging along. Many people have a difficult time in the market because they try to approach it in a manner that is at odds with their personality. A highly emotional person struggles with a measured approach, and an impulsive person has a hard time with a calm, methodical style.

There are longtime traders and emotional traders, but very few longtime emotional traders. Some seem to make their strong emotions work for them, but they are the exception, not the rule. I imagine that highly emotional investors have learned to channel their emotions appropriately so that their emotions don't lead them too far astray. If you aren't an emotional type, you need to work extra hard to keep your emotions in check and not be overly influenced by every little swing in the market. Stay aware of your biases, tendencies, preferences, and habits. Some of them can be quite positive, but when you fail to see them in yourself, they can be extremely dangerous.

Like many other pursuits, great success in the stock market requires the ability to quickly shift your behavior from one extreme to another. Careful, detailed strategic planning must eventually give way to bold, aggressive action if you want to conquer the market beast. Many people are good at detailed planning, and others are good at acting boldly and decisively, but most of us have to work hard to develop our ability to make a seamless shift from one to the other. The personality types who excel at carefully planning an attack are often too cautious and risk-averse to implement it effectively. Folks who live for aggressive action often find detailed planning and research to be drudgery.

What are your inclinations?

Do you constantly itch to be in the heat of battle, or are you inclined to carefully plan what you might do but are never quite ready to take the plunge? Personally, I need to work harder on my strategic planning. I have a bias toward action, and I constantly have to remind myself to stay patient. Learning to take the ups and downs of investing in stride is an emotional skill that comes with experience. After a while, the ebb and flow of success and failure can be quite comforting. When I go through a bad period, I can shrug it off, because I know it is inevitable that things will eventually turn. I just have to let the cycle play out and keep plugging along.

I tend to be a pretty even-tempered person who doesn't have strong emotional reactions. I take things in stride and take comfort in believing that if I just persist in doing the best I can, things will work out well over time. I work hard to cultivate that thinking in my approach to the market. I try not to be excited about gains or depressed about losses. I seldom worry about missing out on a trade, and I don't dwell on mistakes. The key to success for me is to just keep plugging away through both good and bad. If I allowed my moods to swing with the market, I would not do well.

Investors with more emotional personalities would probably be frustrated if they invested like I did. They have to find a style that works with quick swings in moods, opinions, and emotions. Highly emotional people can be great traders if they learn how to direct and use their emotions to their benefit. There is nothing wrong with being emotional if you are aware of that tendency and use it to your advantage.

Once you understand the emotions that drive you, you can work on developing your style. If you are pessimistic by nature, you'd probably find that shorting is a good approach for you. If you tend to worry a lot, you may do better if you focus on bigger, slower-moving, conservative stocks. If you are a risk-taker who seeks an adrenaline rush, you want to focus on highly volatile small stocks.

The following sections describe a few examples of different styles of Shark Investing that you may want to consider.

Sand Sharks

Sand Sharks are methodical, solitary hunters. They are highly technical and use charts to make decisions. They stick to their money management rules and are highly disciplined. They don't second-guess their system or style and always know what they will do next.

They tend to be pure technicians who block out everything else but what they see on the charts. They know that charts aren't infallible and they deal with that by making sure they use money management systems that prevent them from suffering huge losses. If you prefer to approach the market with a set rule book, this might be the approach for you.

Bull Sharks

Bull Sharks are highly aggressive. They look for action and love to chase the crowd. They focus on what is called momentum or trend following. In momentum or trend following, the goal is to identify the prevailing trend, jump in, ride it for as long as it lasts, and then exit as soon as it looks like it is ending. It is often said that the goal of momentum investors is to "catch the meat of the move."

In a strong rally, the momentum investor buys strength. They tend to prefer stocks that are making new highs. I have found that the way to maximize profits is to stick with the prevailing trend, riding the wave of momentum even when it feels extended and dangerous. The time to run for safety is when things begin to crumble. When breadth slows, support levels erode, and momentum cools, you reduce your risk and protect your gains.

Momentum investing has come to be defined as an approach in which you buy stocks that are breaking important resistance or support levels. The logic is that once a stock breaks out and is in motion, it has a good chance of remaining in motion. The idea is to catch a stock in the early part of a move and ride it as other traders discover the situation and join the trade. It's pretty simple.

A lot of folks fall into the trap of thinking that when traditional momentum isn't working very well, they just need to adjust their approach and find what works better. My response is: Aren't all styles

of trading dependent on momentum to some degree? The only way
to make money in a stock is if it is moving. No momentum means no
movement, so your approach doesn't matter much. Even if you use a
bottom-fishing method of trading or try to catch turning points, you
still need momentum. Identifying a bottom or a turning point is a
good start, but the only way you make any money on the trade is if the
darn thing moves after you catch the bottom.

Nurse Sharks

Nurse Sharks focus on fundamentals and like to hunt from the bottom up. They like to study financial statements and gain confidence
in their investments by knowing the details of the business of the
stocks they invest in.

Investing on a purely fundamental basis is difficult for most individual investors because they have no edge over the giant mutual
funds that have more manpower, better resources, and greater access
to management. Those investors who employ a fundamental style
often face a dilemma when trying to apply an effective money management system: As the price of a stock declines, it might appear to
be an even better bargain. However, if you already have a position,
you can see your losses grow substantially. If it turns out that your
fundamental analysis overlooked something, you can find yourself
quickly buried in a big loss.

On the other hand, good fundamental analysis can add great confidence to your approach to the stock. If you understand what is driving
the price and can take advantage of temporary dislocations, you can
profit greatly. Good fundamental research can help you be more
aggressive when opportunities arise.

Mako Sharks

Mako Sharks are the fastest-moving sharks. The Mako is short-term and moves in and out of positions extremely fast. As a short-term trader, you have to be fast on your feet and take your gains quickly where you have them. The great benefit of this approach is that it limits your chances of losses because you are so quick to exit at the first sign of trouble. The drawback is that you miss out on the really big gains that tend to come when you hold over time.

Adept Mako Sharks can make a good living knocking out steady gains on a small capital base but it isn't easy. It requires complete dedication to the market and a lot of hard work seeking out opportunities. You need to be highly disciplined and adhere to a strict methodology. Good Mako Sharks have the concentration to watch the flow of trading in highly liquid big-cap stocks. I'm much better suited to watching a bunch of stocks in a superficial manner while I constantly troll for new ideas.

Tiger Sharks

Tiger Sharks focus on news and events. They will eat and trade anything. Tiger Sharks use a variety of different approaches, but the essence of what they do is to take advantage of the fleeting price inefficiencies that exist as the market digests significant news and events. The broad market seldom fully recognizes or appreciates the true value of new developments, and that is where Tiger Sharks make their money. Tiger Sharks watch the news wires, scan SEC filings, and closely monitor quarterly earnings reports. They move with lightening speed and are willing to bet on either market underreactions or overreactions.

This approach requires quick action and can be dangerous if you are too aggressive and are caught on the wrong side of a trade, but it can be extremely lucrative when you come across the right opportunities.

Hammerhead Sharks

Hammerhead Sharks have their eyes set far apart. This gives them enhanced senses, which they use to anticipate future events. Hammerheads are constantly trying to guess exactly when the market will make a turn, and they look to jump in front of significant market-moving events.

There are two basic ways to approach the market: Either you run with the crowd and play the prevailing momentum, or you use the crowd as a contrary indicator to tell you when things are so extreme that a turn is likely. Hammerheads are contrarians. They are always looking to go against the crowd and like to be negative when everyone else is positive, and vice versa.

This is a tough approach and tends to used more by the big, slow-moving Whales than by the small, flexible, individual investor. Trying to catch turns and guess how events will turn out can be dangerous, but it can pay off extremely well when you are right.

Whale Sharks

Whale Sharks are bigger investors who manage large amounts of capital but realize the benefits of the Shark Investing methods. They understand they have to modify the basic Shark Investing strategies because they cannot move as quickly and lack some flexibility. But they maintain the Shark Investing mind-set and attempt to stay in control and be reactive to the market. The more capital you have to manage, the more likely it is that you will have to adopt a longer-term passive approach. But you can use portions of your capital in a Shark Investing fashion and use elements of Shark Investing no matter how big you are.

Great White Sharks

Great White Sharks are the most deadly of all the sharks. They amalgamate the skills of many different sharks and develop a truly unique and personal style that suits their abilities, emotions, and personalities. The Great White combines chart reading, momentum, reactions to news, and a variety of other things in various quantities to arrive at a market-beating style.

The essence of Great Whites is that they are in tune with what they do best, and they do it aggressively. Nothing is more likely to produce great results than enjoying what you do and doing it with great vigor.

Endnote

1. Landon Thomas, Jr., and Carol Vogel, *New York Times*, March 3, 2005.

13

Putting It All Together

We have covered quite a bit of ground very quickly. I expect it will take some time and some contemplation before you can fully integrate the Shark Investing approach into your thought process and make it your own. That's a good thing. Fundamental changes in how we view something should not come too easily. We need to work through the logic and fully debate it in our mind before we can appreciate its true value and fully embrace it. It should be quite clear that Shark Investing isn't just a set of simple rules. It is a fundamental way of thinking about and dealing with the market. Hopefully you already feel more in control of your investing and are thinking about the stock market in a whole new light.

Your job now is to put this new and powerful thought process to work. What steps should you take to make the Shark Investing style work for you?

Proper Tools

First, make sure you have all the tools you need to be successful. As we discussed in Chapter 8, "Implementing the Shark Investing Style," you need a good online broker, a charting service, and a place to obtain

news and fundamental data about stocks, such as Yahoo! Finance or
Google Finance.

Clear the Deck

Next it is often a good idea to clear the deck and get rid of your bag-
gage. If you have been lugging some poor-performing stocks for a
while, it can be refreshing and empowering to dump them and start
with a clean slate. Many investors fail to appreciate that a fresh start is
available any time they want simply by selling stocks. Instead, they
continue to dwell on problems and mistakes of the past and let their
precious capital stagnate in stocks that they hold on to for emotional
reasons rather than financial ones. When you sell everything and are
working with cash, it is much easier to attack the market in a new and
different way than you had in the past.

Develop a Steady Stream of New Ideas

You are now ready to dive in and try out your investing fins, but how
do you come up with some good ideas to start with?

Many investors produce mediocre returns simply because they
don't have any new ideas. They just stick to the same old stocks that they
have focused on for years. Often we feel a certain loyalty to a stock that
has rewarded us well in the past. But stocks tend to have a limited life
span in which they produce their best returns; eventually they all slow
down. You need to move on to new ideas if you want to continue racking
up big gains.

Shark Investors develop a stock "hunting" methodology. The
search for new ideas is part of their standard investing routine.
The importance of this concept is often overlooked. We figure that
the stocks we are holding are pretty good, so we don't expend the

effort to keep looking for even better ideas. If you make the hunt for new ideas part of your regular routine, you will escape the danger of becoming complacent with the stocks you are holding.

The most important component of any stock-hunting methodology is to do a lot of reading. You can read stock message boards, newspapers, newsletters, and websites and come up with some pretty good lists of stocks to follow. In many cases, it is just a matter of reading widely and making notes of things that have interesting stories. Quite often, reading helps me identify an "investing theme" such as China-related stocks, solar energy stocks, Internet stocks, mining stocks, or whatever. After I have identified an interesting theme, I look for stocks that are in that group, create a number of watch lists, and start doing some research.

Many resources on the Web help you research stocks. For example, theStreet.com and RealMoney.com, where I write a daily stock market commentary, have dozens of market pros providing ideas for you to consider.

Many other sites are available, but the amount of information can be so overwhelming that at times it is easy to feel lost. Don't worry about that too much. Make some long lists of stocks that look interesting; you can narrow it down later. The key is to have a good selection to start with so that you can find the handful that will turn out to be the winners.

At my website, SharkInvesting.com, I expand on the Shark Investing theory and concepts, provide a real money sample portfolio, and offer lists of new ideas. The many participants on the site also offer their ideas and insights. A quick review of the resources on the site will give you a good list of stocks that you may want to look at more closely.

Once you become more sophisticated, another approach to finding good ideas is to use screening software. A number of programs allow you to scan the entire universe of stocks for certain fundamental and/or technical characteristics.

I use one such scanning service called Daily Graphs Online. This service is offered by *Investor's Business Daily* and uses its proprietary ranking system for stocks. This scanning system lets me sort my stocks in a number of ways. For example, I might look for stocks that are priced between 10 and 20, have had large increases in volume, have good relative strength compared to the broader market, and are trading within 20% of their highs. This would yield a good list of stocks that I could then look at more closely.

Narrow Down Your List

Now that you have a list of stocks to work with, you need to narrow it down and find the best potential candidates. You will want to consider the chart, the fundamentals, and news of each stock.

The most important consideration is the chart. You can have great fundamentals and exciting news, but if the stock isn't acting right, you don't want to waste your time. Keep in mind that the chart tells you the real story about a stock's health. If it isn't attracting buyers and showing some strength, it's probably because someone big knows something that the broad market doesn't.

Deciding which stocks have charts that justify further research is something that requires practice. Typically I look for bases and support and up trends and things that indicate that there is some buying momentum. The key is to look at the chart and consider the emotions that are likely in play and the likelihood that someone may know something about the company that is not common knowledge.

The best way to become adept at chart reading is to look at lots and lots of charts. Professional investors look at hundreds of charts each day. When you do that, you can't help but begin to understand what patterns and formations are likely to lead to favorable action.

Keep in mind that chart reading is much more an art than a science and is an imperfect art at best. Even the best-looking charts sometimes fail to act as you expect. That is why the money management rules discussed in Chapter 10, "Portfolio Management: The Key to Success," are so important. Identifying a good chart is no guarantee that the stock will cooperate. Good charts just increase your odds of success.

Now that you have culled your list and are focusing on stocks with favorable charts, you need to look at fundamentals. It is helpful to have a basic understanding of the business a company is in just so you know if it might benefit from being in a favorable sector. For example, I recently was considering a small mining stock. The chart looked good, and when I looked at the fundamentals, I discovered that the company had started mining uranium. The uranium sector had recently attracted much interest, and as the broader market came to recognize that this company was also in that sector, it was likely to benefit as well.

As discussed in Chapter 11, "Fundamental Analysis: Quick and Easy Is All You Need," the idea is to do some fast and easy research to see if earnings and revenues are growing and to quickly measure how expensive or cheap the stock might be.

Quite often you will come across stocks that are extremely strong but appear quite expensive. In these cases the market is obviously anticipating some good news down the road that might not yet be reflected in the analyst estimates. These types of stocks can make very powerful moves, but they also are quite dangerous, especially when a strong market suddenly turns down. If you play these stocks, it is important to have a plan of attack and to be ready to exit quickly should trouble develop.

Start Stalking Your Prey

You now have a good list of promising looking stocks to consider, but you don't want to just jump in blindly. You want to track them for a little while, get to know their personalities, and decide on a plan of attack.

Quite often I take a small initial position in a stock that looks interesting to focus on it and to make sure that I don't lose track of it.

It is important to keep in mind that stocks usually don't go straight up or straight down. They will give you numerous opportunities for good entries. As you follow your starting position, you should get a sense of this and be able to identify potential areas where you might want to begin accumulating more shares.

If the starting position doesn't work the way you hoped, dump it and move on. Don't try to force an investment just because you've spent some time looking at a particular stock. You have to stay selective and cut the pretenders without mercy. The only good stock is one that makes you money.

Plan the Attack, and Make Your Move

After you have stalked your prey for a while and are satisfied with how it is acting, it is time to plan your attack. At this point you want to consider if news such as an earnings report is scheduled to be released. News can quickly turn a good stock into a bad one. Nothing is worse than buying a stock one day only to be hit with bad earnings news the next. Make sure that no surprises are lurking about that might impact your stock.

At this point you want to contemplate what is going on in the broader market. About 70% of what moves a stock is the overall market. If the market is going down, it is harder for many stocks to go higher. There are always exceptions to the rule, but in general you want to have the market winds at your back. The state of the overall market will influence how aggressive you will want to be. If you are concerned that the market might be turning down, you may want to alter your attack plans and start with a small position. In a strong market you may want to be more aggressive at an early point.

Before you jump in and make your buy, have a plan in place. Here are the questions your plan of attack should address:

- What is my time frame for this investment?
- Do I want to hold this stock both long- and short-term?

- How big of a position do I want for each time frame?
- How many partial buys should I make, and over what time period?
- Within what price ranges am I looking to make buys?
- At what key levels should I start to cut my losses?
- How much time do I give this investment to produce results?
- At what price do I start to take some profits?

You now know what you want to do, and you stay patient and wait for the conditions you want. You add to your small starter position and then watch the chart for further development. You know you want to add further shares at some point, but you stay patient and give the stock some time. Finally, when you see the stock do what you want, you jump in much more aggressively and add to your position.

One of the big mistakes many investors make is not being aggressive enough when the time is right. It can be quite difficult to shift from being patient to taking aggressive action. But you must do so if you really want to capitalize on the good opportunities you find. My biggest regrets are typically the good stocks I found but failed to attack in an aggressive fashion when the time was right. Patience and caution must give way to aggressive action at some point if you truly want to earn some money.

Manage the Investment

Now that you have established your position, it is time to manage it and make sure the stock is doing the job you hired it to do. As discussed in Chapter 10, don't be afraid to use selling as a form of insurance should the stock start to act in a worrisome way. Sometimes paring back a position, rather than selling the whole thing, is the way to go when the action looks dicey, but the key here is not to be passive.

Shark Investors don't buy a stock and forget it. They are demanding and require that it produce results for them by a certain time. Something in the market is always going up, and that is where we want to be.

Sell and Move On

All stocks have a limited period of time in which they produce their best results. It may be a few years or even just a few months, but the big moves never last forever. Shark Investors know this and move on to the next opportunity after they have had a good run with a stock.

Too often investors develop a loyalty to a stock that has performed well for them in the past. For example, many folks did quite well with stocks like Dell and Cisco in the late 1990s. But rather than take their gains, they stuck with them long after they made their big moves. Save your love and warm feelings for family and friends. Stocks won't ever love you back. They owe no loyalty even to those who have treated them well.

Repeat the Process

Eventually you will have a number of good investments going, but the most important thing is to keep looking for more and better ones. Shark Investors are never satisfied with their holdings. They are always looking for something better and are prepared to cut their weakest holdings as soon as they find something with more promise.

Patience and Persistence

One of the things about the stock market that can be frustrating is that hard work doesn't necessarily result in immediate financial payoff.

There is no clear correlation between effort and profit. Sometimes it seems like you have the magic touch, and anything you buy ends up doing well. At other times, no matter how much you research, analyze, and study, nothing seems to work.

In most jobs, the harder you work, the better you do. The correlation is direct and immediate. In the stock market there is a correlation over the long term as your skills improve, but in the short run there are no guarantees that brute effort will result in any advantage.

The solution is to simply be cognizant of the nature of the market and to acknowledge that hard work doesn't always result in immediate gain. However, in the long run, the harder you work, the better you will become at capitalizing on the market when it is cooperating. One thing you also will learn is that the harder you work, the more luck you will have over time.

It is important to keep in mind the power of persistence. Some of the best investors I know aren't great stock pickers, technicians, or market seers. They just don't give up, no matter how hard it gets. Like the stock market itself, the nature of investing is cycles of good and bad. You have to put up with the bad so that you can enjoy the good when it finally arrives. The worst thing you can do is give up when things look bleak. As sure as the sun rises and the seasons change, there will come a time when things will brighten and you will wonder why you allowed yourself to feel so much anguish about the market.

Don't let unrewarded effort in the short term keep you from doing the hard work that is needed to be a successful Shark Investor in the long run. If you stick with it long enough and work hard enough, I guarantee you will be successful.

The Sharkfolio Example

On my website at SharkInvesting.com, I demonstrate the concepts in this book in real time using a real money portfolio called the Sharkfolio.

The Sharkfolio was instated on November 23, 2004 when I deposited $100,000.00 in a brokerage account at E✳Trade. On June 22, 2007 the portfolio had grown to $203,014.00. That represents a gain of 103% versus the S&P 500, which gained 27.7% during the same period of time.

The Sharkfolio is an easy and convenient way to begin your journey to becoming a Shark Investor. It is only through the actual application of the Shark Investing principles with real money on the line that you will be able to fully appreciate how and why this approach works.

14

Learning Is a Never-Ending Process

Shark Investing is like most good things in life. If it were simple to master and easy to do well, it wouldn't be so potentially lucrative. The fact that it requires some study, contemplation, and effort, and isn't just a get-rich-quick scheme is why it holds genuine potential to reward you well.

No simple and easy way to make money in the market ever works for long. Highly sophisticated and aggressive investors will always find a way to exploit simple mechanical approaches to the market and ruin them. If we know we can consistently make money by buying at noon on Monday and selling at noon on Thursday, more and more other investors become aware of this as well. To maximize their advantage, they will try to buy a little earlier and sell a little earlier to get a jump on the others who are using this same system. Eventually the pattern that existed will disappear, because too many people are aware of it and are looking for ways to exploit it and gain a better edge.

That tendency of the market to exploit the obvious is what undermines the profitability of any simple and easy system. This doesn't mean you can't find systematic ways to make good money. It does mean you have to respect the fact that it will be challenging and that you will have to constantly adapt as market conditions change.

That is why Shark Investing is not a simple set of rules, but a mind-set. It is complicated at times, and you must keep in mind that it is impossible to "master" the market. Regardless of how competent you are, the market will always find ways to humble you. The minute you think you know it all, I guarantee you that the market will find a way to make you feel foolish.

Great investors understand that they must always be learning new things, seeking greater understanding, and looking to gain deeper insights. The investing process is a fascinating one. Think of it as being similar to a game of chess, where you are always trying new ideas and gambits to gain an edge. Embracing the challenge of constantly trying to improve your skills is what helps make you a better and more successful investor. The highest-performing professionals in any field are perpetual students and are always looking for ways to improve their skills.

Gaining competency as a Shark Investor not only requires study and thought but also is an emotional commitment. Not only do you have to understand the theories and concepts, but you need the fortitude to act on them. Only by applying the Shark Investing principles to the market over a longer period of time do you really learn the most important lessons. It is important to go through a number of market cycles of ups and downs so you are battle tested under all conditions. As the old saying goes, everyone is a genius in a bull market when all you have to do is buy and hold.

Great investing success comes only after you understand the heart and soul of your investing methodology—and that can take some time. Even then, you will go through periods of time when things don't work well. The key is persistence. You have to keep plugging away day after day and not become discouraged when things don't go your way. Even the best investors have runs when nothing goes right, but they know if they keep working at it, things will eventually start falling into place again.

Developing a Gut Feeling

Although my gut definitely isn't in the best physical condition, I have come to respect its mental abilities. When my gut tries to tell me something, I listen carefully and tend to act on it even if I'm not sure why I should.

That is a function of being in the investing game for a long time and having learned thousands of lessons with my hard-earned money. I can't even begin to articulate what many of those lessons are, but they become part of how you think and feel and see the market. They lead you in the right direction more often than not.

It is easy to use gut feelings as a way to circumvent logical thinking and rigid discipline. But with time and experience, you learn when those feelings are valid and when they are a product of other forces or inclinations you should overlook.

It's easy to let outside issues impact your feelings. You must be careful to separate those from your true feelings about the market alone. Over time gut feeling will become one of your most valuable tools, but it can be a dangerous one until you have the experience to fully appreciate it.

Measuring Success

It is easy to measure financial success in the market. Everyone knows how much money they have made or lost. However, even if you are unhappy with your returns, you have not failed if you have learned and grown from the experience. You have failed only if you continue to do the same things that produced poor returns in the past.

One of the great things about the market is that it is such a worthy opponent. The Market Beast always presents a formidable challenge. No matter how good or experienced you may be, the battle is never won. You must constantly strive to improve your investing skills yet not be frustrated by the fact that the job will never be finished and you will never be perfect. No matter how good you are, Mr. Market will beat you quite often.

It is important to maintain a healthy respect for the Market Beast's skill, persistence, and cunning. As soon as you think you have it figured out, the market will find a way to bite you.

As you review your progress as a Shark Investor on a regular basis, be sure you focus not only on returns but also on the confidence you have gained and the feeling of control that you now have. Eventually those feelings will serve you well. You must always appreciate the difficulty of the battle ahead, but also be sure you take pleasure in doing your best, improving your skills, and working hard at one of the toughest games of all.

It can be helpful to set financials goals for yourself so that you stay intently focused on the bottom line. Ultimately that is all that matters, and you will find that, if you have concrete goals, you will work harder at finding ways to attain them. When goals are too vague, it's easy to let your day slide without putting forth the effort you are capable of.

Recommended Reading

Confessions of a Street Addict, Jim Cramer, 2002.

How I Made $2,000,000 in the Stock Market, Nicolas Darvis, 1986.

How to Make Money in Stocks: A Winning System in Good Times or Bad, William J. O'Neil, 2002.

How to Trade in Stocks: The Livermore Formula for Combining Time, Element and Price, Jesse Livermore and Richard Smitten, 1940, 2001.

Investor Therapy: A Psychologist and Investing Guru Tells You How to Out-Psych Wall Street, Richard Geist, 2003.

Japanese Candlestick Charting Techniques: A Contemporary Guide to the Ancient Investment Techniques of the Far East, Steve Nison, 2001.

Puzzles of Finance: Six Practical Problems and Their Remarkable Solutions, Mark P. Kritzman, 2000.

Reminiscences of a Stock Operator, Edwin Lefevre, 1923, 1994.

The Winner's Curse: Paradoxes and Anomalies of Economic Life, Richard Thaler, 1994.

The Wisdom of Crowds: Why the Many Are Smarter Than the Few and How Collective Wisdom Shapes Business, Economies, Societies and Nations, James Surowiecki, 2004.

Why Smart People Make Big Money Mistakes and How to Correct Them: Lessons from the New Science of Behavioral Economics, Gary Belsky and Thomas Gilovich, 2000.

www.SharkInvesting.com and www.RealMoney.com.

I am quite proud of my personal website, SharkInvesting.com. With the help of a number of very smart investors I have worked with over the years, we provide a forum that offers education, investing ideas, market commentary, and a real money portfolio where I demonstrate Shark Investing theories. The site also has a lively community of Shark Investors who share ideas and insights on a daily basis.

In addition to SharkInvesting.com, I write regular market commentary on RealMoney.com. This site offers articles and commentary from many other market professionals, including the legendary Jim Cramer.

15

Investing/Trading as a Career

Over the years I've worked in a wide variety of jobs—lawyer, CPA, CEO, janitor, ice cream vendor, lawn mower salesman, pizza maker, busboy. But nothing I've ever done has been as interesting and enjoyable as investing in the stock market. Initially, the main appeal of being a professional investor was simply the flexibility and freedom it gave me.

Just being my own boss gave me great satisfaction, but what really made a big difference was that I enjoyed the work so much. It quickly became clear that being an investor was the right fit for me. To wake up and look forward to what I would do that day made a huge difference not only in my happiness but ultimately in my paycheck as well. The market can often be incredibly frustrating, but if you stick with it, the rewards can far exceed your boldest expectations. There aren't many businesses where you have a fresh set of great opportunities to start every day.

If the idea of becoming a full-time investor/trader appeals to you, the first thing you have to consider is how much capital you need to get started. This is hard to determine, because there are so many subjective considerations. Not only do you need sufficient capital to invest and trade, but you also need enough to cover your living costs when you go through the inevitable slumps. You never know how long those may last.

Some folks might need to earn $200,000 a year just to cover their living costs, whereas someone else may have a working spouse or other income sources and need almost nothing.

Whatever your situation might be, you want to make sure your living costs are covered for at least one year. Assuming that you are not a novice, one year should be long enough for you to assess whether you are cut out to be a professional investor/trader. Of course, if the market happens to trend in one direction the entire time, you may not be able to evaluate your long-term ability to handle all sorts of different markets—and that is the key. You have to learn how to prosper in a variety of markets. A lot of folks are geniuses when stocks are in a strong rally, but the real test comes when things are choppier or in a downtrend.

Assuming that your living costs are covered by either separate savings or other sources of income, how much capital do you need to dedicate to investing or trading to make a go of it? The answer depends in large part on your style. The shorter your time frame and the greater your turnover, the less capital you probably need. A longer-term trading or investing style usually requires greater capital, because you do not turn over your capital as quickly.

The real dilemma here is that if you are trading ultra-short-term, you can probably get away with quite a bit less capital, but you have a greater chance of unprofitable churning. The more capital you have, the more patient you can be with a variety of stocks. Investors with limited capital who are trying to generate some fast gains often find themselves being slowly nibbled to death by minor losses. If you are working with larger amounts of capital, you have a greater margin for error and can afford to wait longer for a trade to work in the manner you hope.

I'm not suggesting that a longer-term time frame is always safer, but having enough capital so that you can be patient with trades and stay diversified to some degree is a major advantage. Being forced to sell just to move money elsewhere can be quite costly.

All of this is my long-winded way of saying you probably need a minimum of $200,000 to $500,000 in capital before you should try quitting your job and investing or trading full time. That allows you to diversify your holdings a bit and takes the sting out of transaction costs. The more capital you have, the more patient you can be, and patience is often the key to success. Remember, there are no guarantees. If your timing is poor and you hit a difficult market, you may not succeed even though you possess the requisite skill. It certainly is possible to start with less capital, but there is less margin for error and much more pressure to produce results quickly. That can add an element of stress that will make success even more difficult.

Another highly personal consideration is how easily you can return to a paying job should professional investing/trading not work out for you. If finding a new job will be an issue, you better make sure you have a big cushion before you quit your present job.

If you work hard at it, enjoy learning new things, have reasonable expectations, and are adequately capitalized, professional investing is one of the best ways I can think of to earn a living.

Here is a question that someone recently asked me: "I decided to become a full-time investor two months ago. I have lost about $10,000 so far, and I am becoming discouraged. The people I talk with say that I've had bad luck and started trading at the wrong time, and that it usually takes about six months to start making money. Do you think I should stick with it (I love it so much), or should I face the fact that I stink, and go back to my old job?"

My answer was that I think it is premature to conclude that you "stink" at trading after only two months. Trading skill can be measured only over the long term because of the impact that luck—both good and bad—has on results over a short period of time. Only after you have been through a variety of market environments and have confronted bull runs and bear raids can you determine if you can earn a living this way.

Keep working on developing your unique style of investing or trading. The key is to find an approach that meshes with your personality. Traders often feel that they have to be able to make consistent profits in all environments to be successful. That is not true. You just have to be able to profit big when conditions are in your favor. The fact that you "love the market" is a major advantage. As long as you have capital, are persistent, and constantly strive to learn and grow, you have a good chance of a successful career as an investor/trader.

The worst thing that can happen to most new investors is to have immediate success. It is easy to think you are an investing prodigy when all that really has happened is a run of beginner's luck. One of the best early lessons you can learn is that the market is difficult and that it requires constant effort over a long period of time to firmly establish yourself. Another thing to keep in mind is that most investing styles do not yield profits in a steady and consistent manner. You will probably find that you will have long periods with little progress and then a quick burst of profits.

Although you may have a short time frame when it comes to your investments, you need to be in the game for the long haul. The key to success in investing is not necessarily market insight or good stock-picking (although they help), but persistence. You have to stick with it and have staying power during the bad times. If you can stick it out during the bad times, you will surely enjoy some good times.

Investors who do not recognize up front that there will be some very trying times when they can't do anything right are doomed to fail. Only after you recognize and embrace the boom-and-bust cycle of most investing approaches can you prosper as a professional investor. Full-time investing is a great way to earn a living, but if you aren't prepared for the long haul and can't handle disappointment, this is not a good career option for you.

Aside from monetary matters, probably the most important thing to consider is your emotional and psychological makeup. Ultimately your emotions determine your level of success as an investor. The most important emotional quality for investors is to be balanced. You need to be confident yet cautious, flexible but not wishy-washy, analytical but intuitive, egotistical but humble. Good investors need a bit of ego so that they can act with confidence and conviction, but they also have to be very humble and willing to admit to mistakes and errors in judgment on a regular basis. One of the key qualities for success is to be able to control your emotions as the market moves. You can't become overly euphoric when things are going well or overly depressed when your luck is running bad. Steady objectivity while those around you lose control is a great benefit.

It is also important that your style of investing or trading conform to your emotional strengths. Temperament plays a big part in how comfortable you are with a particular investing style. A good technical trader, for example, will have a different mind-set and emotional makeup than an investor who focuses primarily on fundamentals. Some folks simply don't feel comfortable buying a stock unless they do plenty of research first. Others will buy a stock without even knowing the company name. There are folks who operate best when they fight the crowd and prevailing sentiment rather than run with them. Other folks, like me, do best when we catch momentum and ride it.

There are many ways to make your emotions work for you, but no matter how you approach the market, balance is tremendously important. Investors who can walk the thin line between emotional extremes produce consistently good results. If you are serious about being a full-time investor, you must be sure that you can handle a variety of market conditions. It sure feels good when you trounce the averages and double your account in a bull run, but that isn't enough to deem yourself capable of making a living full-time in the stock market.

Here are some questions you need to ask yourself: Am I mentally and psychologically capable of handling a trading slump of many months? Can I adapt if market conditions render my trading style impotent? Can I handle the isolation of being a solitary trader working alone? Do I have the self-discipline to be my own boss? Do I have reasonable expectations? Can I deal with technical difficulties of any sort that will surely plague and frustrate me?

A full-time job as an investor is a great way to make a living, but it isn't for everyone. Many people, if not most, will fail at it. However, the good news is that it is easy to get started on a part-time basis and to experiment and try a few things on the side without giving up your present job. If you are serious about being a full-time investor, dive in and get to work right now. If you are cut out for it, you will find out soon enough.

Glossary of Useful Terms and Concepts

See Chapter 14, "Learning Is a Never-Ending Process," for useful books and websites.

analysis paralysis

Becoming so overwhelmed with researching details that you become confused and incapable of taking action. There is a similar condition I call **timing torpidity**, in which you are so involved in trying to time the exact turning point in the market that you lose perspective and end up doing little.

averaging down

Adding to an existing position at a price below what you had paid previously. Quite often this is done in an emotional manner rather than as part of a systematic plan and should be avoided.

averaging in

Adding to an existing position at prices higher or lower than what you had paid previously. This usually involves using a stock's normal volatility to establish a new position over time and is done as part of a systematic plan.

blow-off top/capitulation low

When emotions become so extreme and investors rush to act on them, it often produces a turning point in the market. When the emotional extreme occurs at the bottom, it is called a capitulation low. Typically it manifests itself as panic, with investors looking to escape the market at any cost. That frenzy of selling exhausts the sellers and the market turns back up. The crash in 1987 is a classic example of a capitulation low. When the opposite occurs on the upside, it is called a blow-off top or **capitulation top**. This typically occurs following a period of increased speculation when, in one final frenzy of buying, folks with cash on hand simply can't take the pain of watching the market move without them any longer. They finally say, "The heck with this; I'm joining the party," and throw their money at any stock that is moving. That exhausts the buying and the market reverses downward.

bull trap

Occurs when a stock or index makes a clear technical break that forces short sellers to cover and sucks in the money on the sidelines. After everyone is in and ready for the ride straight up, we quickly reverse and trap the newly minted bulls' capitulation, the point where the disbelievers can't take it anymore and decide to give up and join the prevailing trend.

Cockroach Theory

Problems, like cockroaches, seldom come in isolation. If a company has one problem, you can bet that others are lurking about to surprise you. Quite often it is better to dump a stock at the first sign of problems rather than wait for the other cockroaches to show themselves.

Elliott Wave Theory

A theory that says that markets' primary moves takes place in five-wave patterns, and corrections occur in three-wave patterns, much like waves on the beach as the tide is coming in.

ETF

Exchange-traded fund. A convenient vehicle that allows investors to buy or sell an index. **Spyders** (SPY:Amex), which mimics the **S&P 500**, started trading in 1988. The **Nasdaq 100 Trust** (QQQ:Amex), which mimics the **Nasdaq 100**, began trading in 1989. **Diamonds** (DIA:Amex), which reflects the **Dow Jones Industrial Average**, was a latecomer that didn't start trading until 1998.

fade the move

Occurs when traders position themselves in anticipation that the prevailing move in the market will suddenly end and reverse. For example, when the market opens strongly on a Monday morning many traders will sell into that strength because they don't expect it to last. They are "fading the move."

fading

A style of trading fast-moving televised stock picks. Fading recognizes that the price action in stocks mentioned on television is seldom sustained. It has a very limited life span as traders rush in and out and then move on to their next play.

Fibonacci numbers

Are used in technical analysis to determine a logical turning point for stocks. The idea behind Fibonacci numbers is that a certain flow exists in nature that consistently produces a certain mathematical pattern. The pattern is seen in such things as waves, honeybees, flower petals, human anatomy, and so on. The pattern is 0,1,1,2,3,5,8,13,21, and so on, where each succeeding number is the sum of the two immediately preceding. This is applied to charts and is used to help find a point where a stock might reverse up or down.

front running

A style of trading fast-moving televised stock picks. Front running is trying to guess what will be mentioned ahead of time, or being extremely quick in buying once there is a mention. The idea is to be properly positioned as slower traders rush in and bid up the stock. Once they drive it up a fair amount, the stock is flipped to the late-comers (also called "bag holders"), and the trade is closed.

Hedge fund disease
The irresistible urge to buy stocks that are down sharply in the hope that the selling is "overdone."

January effect
The tendency of stocks that have been pressured by tax-loss selling to bounce back after that selling is completed. The theory is that tax-loss selling pressure relents as soon as the year ends and that allows the stocks to bounce back to "fair" value. This phenomenon is so well-known and anticipated that many investors try to get a jump on it by buying early.

money management
A system whereby you set various rules and parameters by which you allocate your capital to control your losses and gains. The goal is to devise a system so that an unusual run of bad luck will not put you out of business, while at the same time allowing yourself to fully enjoy a run of good luck.

overbought/oversold
Market commentators often use the terms overbought and oversold to describe the market's condition. Unfortunately, they are generally used in a rather vague manner. More often than not, these terms simply mean that someone thinks the market has gone up (overbought) or down (oversold) faster than it should. Many market participants are confused by exactly what these terms mean. One common question is, "How can the market be considered oversold after a few days of selling, when it is still up dramatically over the last few months?" Overbought and oversold do have precise technical meanings when

used in conjunction with a stochastic indicator. A stochastic indicator measures where a stock is presently, compared with a specified range. When a stock quickly moves to the top of the range, it is overbought, and when it moves to the bottom of the range, it is oversold. Whether the market is overbought or oversold is a function of time.

program trading
The purchase or sale of a basket of at least 15 stocks with a total value of $1 million or more by one buyer reactive trader, a trader who tends to use a momentum or trend-following approach.

selling the news
When good news is anticipated by traders, a stock will begin to go up in price before the news is actually announced. Once the news is finally announced, its value might already be fully priced in to the stock and those who bought ahead of the news will sell to lock in their gains.

wall of worry
The incremental deployment of buying power in order not to be left on the sidelines is what causes the market to scale the wall of worry, concern, and skepticism.

window dressing
Getting up the price so that the shares you are holding in inventory show a good price. The shares that are actually bought in the effort to do this tend to be irrelevant. Any losses that are taken in the first few days of the new reporting period are shrugged off with the belief that "we'll make it up at the end of the period."

zigzagger
An anticipatory trader. Someone who tries to position himself or herself in front of turning points.

Index

FULL OF BULL
Do What Wall Street Does, Not What It Says, To Make Money in the Market

Stephen T. McClellan

How do you read between the lines, decipher the stock analysts' insider code, put the analysts' research in context, and actually use it to make money? Read *Full of Bull* by Stephen McClellan. For decades, McClellan was one of the Street's leading analysts. He knows exactly how the game is played. In this book, for the first time, he reveals those secrets and deliberate deceptions, putting you on a level playing field with the world's biggest institutional investors. You'll learn how to do what Wall Street does, not what it says; uncover analysts' hidden influences, biases, and blind spots; react appropriately to upgrades, downgrades, and stock price targets; and avoid common errors individual investors make when they use research. Then, drawing on his immense experience analyzing the world's most prominent companies, McClellan shows how to do your own research, systematically evaluate a company's investment prospects, and make investing decisions based on core principles that work. Forthright and bold, *Full of Bull* offers the objective, focused guidance you should be getting from your broker but aren't!

ISBN 9780132360111 ■ © 2008 ■ 240 pp. ■ $25.99 USA ■ $29.99 CAN

TREND FOLLOWING
How Great Traders Make Millions in Up or Down Markets, Expanded Edition (Paperback)

Michael W. Covel

Forewords by Larry Hite, Hite Capital Management, and Charles Faulkner, Market Wizard Trading Coach

How did John W. Henry quietly become rich enough to buy the Boston Red Sox? How have traders like Keith Campbell, Bill Dunn, Jerry Parker, and Salem Abraham consistently generated immense wealth in bull and bear markets? The key is trend following—the only strategy proven to consistently make money. Now, one of the field's leading experts shows how it works and how you can take advantage of it. Michael Covel reveals the "underground" network of little-known traders and hedge fund managers who've been using trend following for decades. He introduces its fundamental concepts and techniques, and, using 100 pages of easy-to-understand charts from top trend followers, he shows why only a technical system based on following price trends can win over the long term. Covel presents more than a decade's worth of data and shows even more backtested trend following results, so you can gain greater confidence in the method. Along the way, Covel thoroughly debunks misinformation and failed advice from pros who ought to know better. This timely book capitalizes on today's intense volatility and uncertainty to give investors what they're desperately searching for: a strategy that really works.

ISBN 9780136137184 ■ © 2007 ■ 448 pp. ■ $17.99 USA ■ $20.99 CAN